# A Kid's Guide to Fly Tying

# A Kid's Guide to Fly Tying

Tyler Befus

JOHNSON BOOKS
BOULDER

Published by Johnson Books, a Big Earth Publishing company.
1637 Pearl Street, Suite 201, Boulder, Colorado 80302.
1-800-258-5830
E-mail: books@bigearthpublishing.com
www.bigearthpublishing.com

Cover and text design by Rebecca Finkel
Edited by Kira McFaddon

9   8   7   6   5   4   3   2   1

Library of Congress Cataloging-in-Publication Data
Befus, Tyler.
A kid's guide to fly-tying / By Tyler Befus.
p.  cm.
ISBN 978-1-55566-425-1
1. Fly tying—Juvenile literature.  I. Title.
SH451.B373 2008
799.12'4—dc22
2008033075


Printed in China

*I dedicate this book to my dad, Brad Befus.*

He took the time to teach me about fly tying

at a very young age. When I tie a couple of new flies,

he always makes the time to take me fishing

so I can see if they work. He also takes me to flyfishing

and fly-tying shows all over the country

so I can keep learning more.

Thank you so much, dad, for all the support and love.

—TYLER

# Contents

# Foreword By Bob Jacklin

It has been very refreshing for me to meet, fish with, and get to know several young boys in the past several years who love the outdoors and flyfishing. These boys are developing a passion for the sport of flyfishing and fly tying. All of them will probably help someday to carry our flyfishing heritage on to another generation. One of these boys is Tyler Befus of Montrose, Colorado. Just eleven years old, Tyler has been flyfishing and tying flies for several years and is becoming quite the young expert in flyfishing, fly casting, and fly tying. It is very much my pleasure to know Tyler and to have fished with him; I am very flattered to be asked to write the foreword for his book.

My Dad gave me one of the most precious gifts a father could give a son—his time! Lisa and Brad Befus are doing just that for their children. They have enabled and encouraged Tyler to pursue flyfishing and all that is related to it. Like many children who are lucky enough to have two dedicated parents, Tyler looks up to and idolizes his parents, as he should. This combination of Tyler's love and dedication to flyfishing and the encouragement and support of his parents have brought to completion this very fine book on fly tying for kids.

Written by Tyler with some help and guidance from his parents, this book gives a slightly different, but straightforward perspective on beginning fly tying. Tyler tries to encourage his audience of young people who are interested in flyfishing to tie their own flies and to experience the joy and satisfaction of catching a fish on a fly that they tied. In short, his message is: "It's fun, it's easy and if I can do it, you can too. So join me as we tie a fly."

Tyler starts with an informative narrative on just what fly tying is, and what the basics of fly tying are. He then describes the tools, hooks, and many of the materials used in fly tying. He moves on to using these items and explaining the various steps in tying materials to the hook. This is a simple yet instructive guide with good photographs and captions. Writing in his own words, Tyler covers tying the dry fly, the wet fly, the nymph, and the streamer fly. He goes on to describe how to use these flies to catch the fish you want.

Tyler finishes up his book with tying instructions for some special flies that the beginner can learn to tie and catch fish with. What more could you ask for? This straightforward book will encourage our young flyfishers to try tying their own flies. It is simply a great beginner's guide to the wonderful world of fly tying. I wish I could have had this book when I was starting to learn this great art.

# Preface

Hi, I'm Tyler Befus. I'm eleven years old and I enjoy flyfishing, playing sports, skateboarding, and piano . . . plus, I'm crazy about tying my own flies! I like tying flies because it provides many adventures, just like flyfishing. You don't have to be a fly fisher to enjoy fly tying, but fly tying will make you a better fly fisher. Generally when we tie flies, we make them imitate bugs and other food items that fish like to eat. Some people like to tie flies that are like artwork, or to tie "realistic flies," which look exactly like a real insect, fish, frog, or crawdad. Some people tie flies to compete in fly-tying competitions, and others just like to tie flies that catch fish.

I began my fly-tying adventures when I was about eighteen months old. My dad would sit me on his lap and let me wrap thread and materials onto a hook. Even though I don't remember that now, except from the pictures, I sure am happy he showed me. Because of this early start, I had the opportunity to be a presenter at my first fly-tying show when I was just three years old. Now, I've traveled all over the country tying flies at flyfishing sport shows and for fishing clubs. In 2006, I had two of my own fly designs accepted to be produced and sold through a company called Umpqua Feather Merchants. By going to different fly-tying shows and events, I've met some really neat friends. Some of them are from places far away like Denmark, Holland, and Japan.

The reason I love fly tying is because there are no boundaries and you can create new flies and be artistic. Fly tying teaches you some great life-long lessons, like patience. Sometimes I get frustrated when I am trying a difficult technique or a tying step on a fly and the whole thing explodes. Well, a fly can't really explode, but sometimes it doesn't work out like I planned. If this happens, I just back up and redo the step to make the fly like I want it.

I decided to write this book so beginners, and especially kids, can learn the basics of fly tying and start their own fly tying adventure. I think there aren't enough kids flyfishing or tying flies, and I want to change that. Learning fly tying may sound hard and a lot like school, but it's an adventure that will teach you about bugs, fly tying techniques, and fly-tying materials. You will make new friends that are also having fun. I hope you enjoy this book and have fun learning to make your own flies!

If you do not know how to flyfish yet or do not understand some of the terms used in this book, you should check out my other book, *A Kid's Guide of Flyfishing* to learn more about flyfishing and the techniques that I refer to in this book.

–Tyler Befus
Montrose, Colorado

# Acknowledgments

I would like to thank my dad for teaching me about fly tying at such a young age, and giving me the knowledge that I needed to write this book. I also thank my mom for taking her time to homeschool me so I can do all these fun and exciting things. I would like to thank Bob Jacklin for writing the foreword for my book. Bob has been an amazing fly-tying instructor for many people for many years, and I cannot think of a better person to write the foreword.

There have been many other people that have helped me out along the way, like my friend Bill Logan from New Jersey, who spent three days teaching me new fly-tying techniques and patterns, and about all kinds of materials. I thank Dr. Whiting and B. J. Lester for allowing me to be on the Whiting Farms Pro Team and for providing me with plenty of incredible fly-tying feathers. Jay Murakoshi taught me how to spin deer hair to make a bass bug, and my good friend Jens Pilgaard from Denmark taught me how to tie a fly in my hands without a vise. Thank you to Bruce Olson at Umpqua Feather Merchants for accepting the fly patterns I created and for selling them to all the fly shops. I also want to thank all the people who have invited me to present for their flyfishing clubs, and all those who have asked me to participate at fly-tying shows, especially Chuck Furimsky, who runs the International Fly-Tying Symposium.

There are so many other fly tiers that I haven't mentioned, and I thank them all for taking the time to show a kid (me) tips on fly tying and share all the life-long lessons they've taught me about this wonderful art and hobby. I also want to thank you, the reader of my book, for your interest in learning more about fly tying.

#  1 What is Fly Tying?

**B**efore we start learning how to tie flies, we need to learn what fly tying is. I believe that fly tying is an art form in which we can create some of our own imitations of insects, fish, and other food items that live in streams, rivers, and lakes. When we tie these imitations we use many interesting and unique materials and tools. We use thread, feathers, fur, beads, flashy stuff, wire, paints, glue, yarn, floss, hair, and a bunch of man-made materials to make flies. There are some things in fly tying that can be challenging at first, but with *practice* you will get it, just like flyfishing. One thing you learn is patience; patience is a key element in fly tying.

Fly tying is a very old activity with a lot of history, just like flyfishing. The first fly ever described in writing was red wool wound on a

You can never practice tying flies too much!

hook with two rooster (male chicken) feathers attached to it. This was written by Aelian (circa 170–230 CE) in his book, *On the Characteristics of Animals.* He describes this pattern and how it was used to catch fish with speckled skin (maybe a trout) in a river in Macedonia.

Flies and fly tying have been described by writers throughout time. Dame Juliana Berners' book *Treatyse of Fysshynge wyth an Angle* was printed in 1496. Izaac Walton (1593–1683) wrote about flies, fly tying, and fly-tying materials in *The Compleat Angler,* first published in 1653. There have been hundreds of books written about fly tying since those early books. Today we're very lucky because we can also find all kinds of information on DVD's, videos, and the Internet.

Today we're very lucky because we can also find all kinds of information on DVD's, videos, and the Internet.

People tie flies for different reasons. Some tie their own flies because it allows them to make flies that they cannot buy in stores. Some tie flies because it's cheaper than buying flies. There are fly tiers that make their living tying flies for the fly shops. There are others who tie flies because they like the art form and might not even flyfish at all. Some fly tiers tie historical flies or classic flies, while others tie super-realistic flies that look like they could crawl or fly right out of their fly-tying vise!

An artistic fly that my dad tied. It's called the Miss Vivian, named after my little sister.

This is a very old wet fly pattern tied by my friend Kyle Hand from Texas.

I'm just as passionate about fly tying as I am about flyfishing. Tying flies allows me to be creative and have fun. When I was about eighteen months old, I would sit on my dad's lap and he would teach me how to wrap the thread on the hook. He showed me how to tie different materials onto the hook to make a tail or a body on a fly. The first fly I tied all by myself was a Woolly Bugger. I was three years old when I tied it. The fly had a yellow tail, a tiger chenille body, and a green hackle, or collar, wound over its body.

There are several basic types of flies—nymphs, wet flies, dry flies, streamers, and poppers.

Here I am getting one of my first fly-tying lessons from my dad.

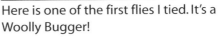

Here is one of the first flies I tied. It's a Woolly Bugger!

This is a traditional wet fly pattern.

## Wet Fly

A wet fly is a fly that imitates a submerged bug or food item. When it hits the water it should sink immediately. When the fly is fished, it can either be drifted in the current to look like a bug drifting, or it can be drifted and then allowed to swing so it looks like a bug that is ready to hatch. It can be stripped, or retrieved, in slow moving or still water to look like a small minnow or a bug that is swimming.

## Nymph

Nymphs are also flies that sink. They usually imitate an aquatic insect that lives under water in lakes, streams, or rivers. They can be made to look like a stonefly, mayfly, caddisfly, midge, damselfly, or dragonfly. There are also nymphs that don't look like any insect, and we call them attractor

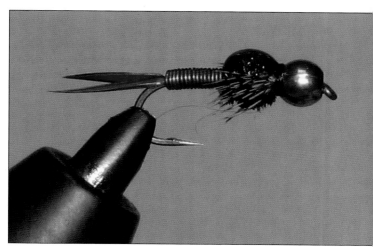

This is a Copper John nymph. It's one of the most well-known flies.

They can be made to look like a stonefly, mayfly, caddisfly, midge, damselfly, or dragonfly.

This is one of my nymphs. It's called Tyler's Fakey Nymph.

nymphs. Nymphs are usually fished by letting them drift naturally in the current just like the real bugs do. This is called drag-free drift.

## Dry Fly

A dry fly is a type of fly that floats to imitate a bug on the surface of the water. This can be a stonefly, caddisfly, mayfly, midge, ant, beetle, grasshopper, or cricket. Dry flies can be fished by letting them drift on the surface of the water drag-

This is a classic dry fly called the Quill Gordon.

free. They can also be skittered on the surface to look like a bug that is trying to fly off the water, or maybe swimming like a grasshopper. There are dry flies that don't look like any one type of insect and we call them attractors.

This dry fly is called a Yellow Humpy.

This is a foam-bodied wasp pattern I learned to tie from my friend Bill Logan.

# Streamer

A streamer is a fly that sinks and imitates a small fish or minnow. In a river, you can let a streamer drift in the current, or let it drift and then swing downstream before stripping it back upstream to look like a small fish swimming. Usually streamers are stripped so that they look

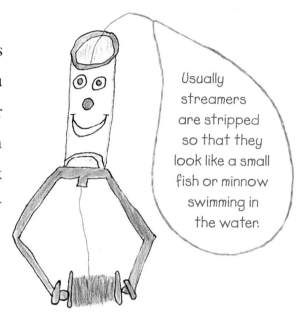

Usually streamers are stripped so that they look like a small fish or minnow swimming in the water.

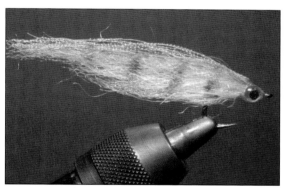

Streamers like this synthetic hair minnow can look very realistic.

Many of the modern streamers use a gold bead or cone on the front for extra weight, like this Squirrely Minnow tied by my dad.

This is a more classic feather wing streamer. I tied this fly for a fly-tying competition in Norway.

like a small fish or minnow swimming in the water. In a lake, you would fish a streamer by stripping the fly back toward you.

## Popper

A popper is a fly that floats on the surface of the water. It is mostly fished in lakes. When the fly is stripped, it pushes the water with a cupped or flat section on its front, causing is to gurgle on the surface of the water make a "popping" sound. Poppers can be made out of foam, deer hair, or plastic.

Poppers can be made out of soft foam like this one, or out of deer hair, cork, or hard foam so they will float.

Tying flies is whatever you want to make out of it. My little sister Vivian likes to tie flies just as long as they are pink or purple.

For me it is so rewarding to catch a nice fish on a fly that I have tied or maybe even created myself!

Here is a close-up view of an artistic fly that I tied. The little details of each fly make tying fun.

# 2 Fly-Tying Tools

Now that we've learned about what fly tying is, we need to learn about some of the tools we use. There are vises, bobbins, scissors, dubbing needles, and more. There are many tools for fly tying, but you don't need all of them. The tools we'll cover in this chapter are the ones that will make tying flies a lot more fun.

## Vises

The first tool is the vise. Its job is to hold the hook securely while we wrap thread, feathers, and fur onto the hook. Vises come in many different styles. Some are very simple and others have a lot of features. One common, featured type is the rotary vise. This vice allows the tier to rotate the hook while it's in the jaws of the vise. It makes it easy to tie on one side of the hook or the

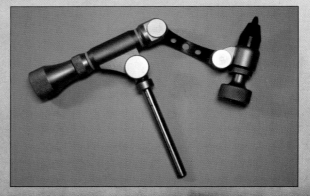

Top: A full rotary vise that spins really fast to wrap materials on the hook. Bottom: This vise rotates and has a lot of different adjustments to help with your tying.

other, or on the bottom of the hook. Some vises have a clamp that attaches to a table or your workbench, while others have a heavy base called a pedestal that sits on the

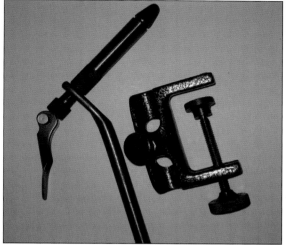

Top: A basic lever-operated vise with a c-clamp to attach to the table. Bottom: A lever-operated vise with some extra features to rotate the hook and change the angle of the jaws.

Top: A spring-loaded jaw system. All you do is squeeze the lever, insert the hook and let go of the lever. Bottom: This is a pedestal-base vise that sits on top of the table instead of clamping to it.

tabletop. In the early days of fly tying, before there were fly-tying vices, people would hold the hook with their fingers.

## Scissors

What you want to look for when you are getting scissors are fine tips, or points, and sharp blades, or edges. Use scissors to trim off extra materials you don't need or want. If your scissors are dull, it can be frustrating. If you're going to cut really bulky or big stuff, you might want to use a second pair of scissors, like the ones you use in school, so you don't dull your good fly-tying scissors. Fly-tying scissors are very sharp and you should always be very careful when you are using them so you do not cut yourself.

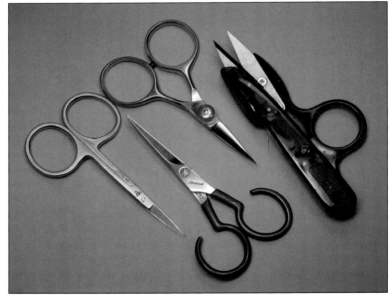

Different types of fly-tying scissors. Some have really fine tips for close-up cutting in small areas. Some are more all-purpose scissors. The one on the right is a sewing-type of scissors. A sharp pair of scissors will make tying much easier and more fun.

## Bobbins

Bobbins hold your tying thread and keep tension on the thread while it hangs from the hook. The bobbin, like the vise, can come with many different features. Some bobbins are spring-loaded, which makes them retract the thread automatically. Others are manual and just keep tension on the thread while it hangs from the hook. Some bobbins have ceramic tubes or ceramic tips so they won't fray the thread. Other bobbins have metal tubes. You only need one bobbin to start tying, but it's nice to have several so you don't have to rethread every time you want to use a different strength or color of thread.

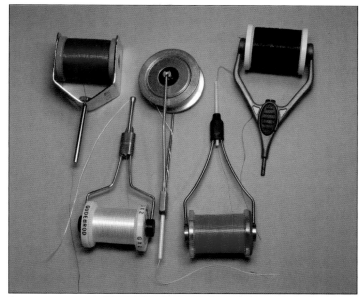

An assortment of bobbins. From left to right: a short bobbin with a metal tube, a standard bobbin with a ceramic tip, an automatic bobbin, a ceramic-tube bobbin, and a plastic bobbin with a ceramic tube.

## Dubbing Needle

A dubbing needle is basically a needle glued into a piece of wood or metal. You can either buy one or make one at home by drilling a hole into a piece

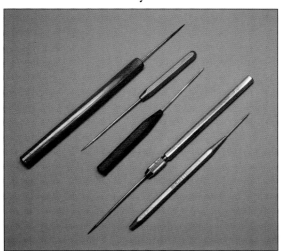

of wood and then gluing a sewing needle into the hole. It's used to pick out materials and to apply glue to the head of your finished flies.

Here are some different dubbing needles. The one on the top I made with my dad. It's a piece of an old bamboo fly rod that we drilled a hole in the end of and glued a sewing needle to.

## Hackle Pliers

Hackle pliers hold feathers and other materials while you wrap them around the hook; it's sort of like having a third hand. To work the pliers, you squeeze them to open the jaws, place the material you want to hold in the jaws and then allow them to close to grab the material. Then you squeeze them when you are done wrapping the material and they will let go of it.

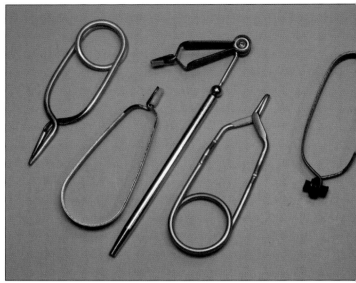

Here are some different styles of hackle pliers. It's important that they hold the material tight while you're wrapping and don't have sharp edges that will break the materials.

## Hair Stacker

The purpose of a hair stacker is to even the tips of deer hair, elk hair, and many other types of hair. You do this when you are making wings or tails. To use a hair stacker, first cut the hair off the

A hair stacker with the tube in the base. Hair is first placed in the tube, then the stacker is tapped on the table. The tube is pulled out and the hair tips are all even for a tail or a wing. We will use a hair stacker later in the book when we tie the Elk Hair Caddis.

hide, then clean out all the fuzzy stuff in the hair with your fingers or with a comb. Next, put the hair into the stacker with the tips of the hair angled down into the stacker. Then hold the stacker in your hand and tap it on a table several times. Hold the stacker on its side and

Hair stacker with the tube removed from the base.

slowly separate the tube from the base. The hair tips will be in the tube, even and ready to be used for wings or tails.

## Light/Lamp

A good light is important because it makes it easier to see where you're tying your materials on the hook. The light should have a very bright bulb so it gives you plenty of light. Your eyes will get tired if you don't have enough light, and it won't be as much fun to tie flies.

Any desk lamp will work just fine. I like lights like this one that have a bright light but don't get too hot.

# Thread

Thread is both a tool and a material. It's the tool that holds materials to the hook, and it's a material that bodies are made out of. There are many different sizes (thickness) and colors of thread available. Most fly-tying threads are made of nylon and are waxed. Understanding thread sizes can be difficult. Below is a simple chart that shows some of the most common thread sizes.

Here are some different colors and types of fly-tying thread. These threads are made just for fly tying and are very strong for their size.

| Thread Size | Thread Use |
| --- | --- |
| 8/0 | This is fine thread used for smaller flies or when you want less bulk. |
| 6/0 | This is a good thread size for most trout flies. |
| 3/0 | This is good for big trout flies, warm-water flies, and some saltwater flies. |
| GSP & KEVLAR | This is super-strong thread used for spinning hair or tying with really bulky materials. |

## Other Tools

There are a lot of other fly-tying tools out there. These are just a few of them:

A **bobbin threader** is used to help get the thread through the tube of the bobbin. **Tweezers** are helpful, and you probably already have some around your house.

**Hackle gauges** measure what size hackle feather you should use for a certain hook size.

Different **knot tiers** called whip finishers help tie the whip-finish knot to complete your flies.

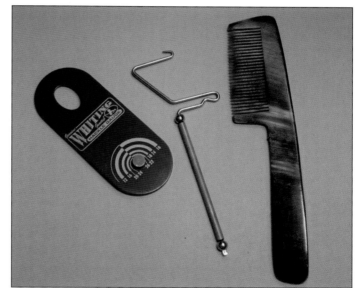

On the left is a hackle gauge, in the middle is a whip-finish tool, and on the right is a comb for combing through deer and elk hair to remove all the fluffy underfur so it's easier to work with and will stack easier in the hair stacker.

# 3 Fly-Tying Hooks and Materials

## Hooks

Hooks come in many different shapes and sizes. Some hooks are straight, while others are curved or bent. The three basic kinds of hooks are dry-fly hooks, wet-fly hooks, and streamer hooks. The wire that forms a dry-fly hook is small to make it float easier. The wire of streamer hooks is heavy, which helps these hooks sink fast. The wire used to make a wet-fly hook, or nymph hook, makes it heavier than a dry-fly hook but not as heavy as a streamer hook. It's important to use a good hook because that's what you're going to build your fly on. Look for a hook that has a good, sharp point and a strong shank. Building a fly on a good hook is like building a house on a good foundation.

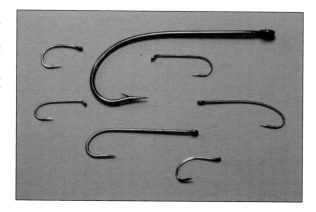

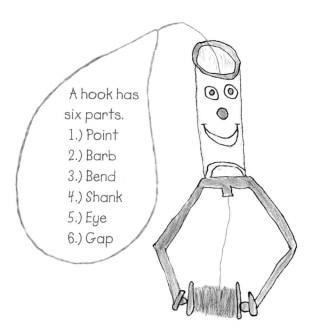

A hook has six parts.
1.) Point
2.) Barb
3.) Bend
4.) Shank
5.) Eye
6.) Gap

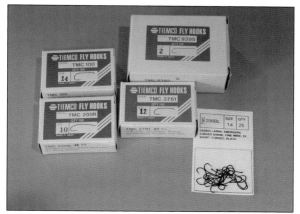

Top: Different types of fly-tying hooks. Center: Some hook packages. Hooks are sold in packages of 100, 50, and 25. Bottom: A close-up view of a hook package showing information about the hooks and their different recommended uses.

Hooks come in many sizes, from very small to really large. We use different sized hooks to match different sized insects, baitfish, and other food items fish eat. The larger the hook size, the smaller the hook. For example, a #12 size hook is smaller than a #4 hook. (*Caution:* Hooks are very sharp and you need to be careful when handling them.)

# Materials
## Feathers

We use many different feathers, including turkey feathers, duck feathers, and chicken feathers. We also use feathers from wild game birds like grouse, pheasant, and partridge. Some feathers we use as wing cases. Others we use as wings and hackles. Feathers can also be used to make tails, or as ribbing to help secure other materials to the hook. Marabou is a type of feather that comes from the underside of a chicken or turkey. Marabou can be used to make a tail, wing, or throat on a fly.

From left to right: chicken feather dyed olive green, Blue Grouse feather, Hungarian partridge feather. All of these feathers are good for tails, legs, and soft hackles on flies that will sink, like nymphs and wet-flies. These feathers are soft and the fibers will move in the water like the legs or tails of a real bug.

From left to right: a mottled turkey wing feather, Ringneck pheasant tail feather. The fibers from these feathers make good tails, legs, and wing cases for flies that will sink because they soak up water easily.

These are rooster saddle feathers for making dry-fly hackles.

These are rooster neck hackles for making dry flies. They come in many different natural and dyed colors.

These are turkey marabou feathers. This is the type of feather we will use to make a tail on a Woolly Bugger and a Soft Hackle Streamer (pages 95, 108). Sometimes they come in bunches like this and are sewn together at the bottom.

This is an individual turkey marabou feather. They are very soft and make our flies come to life when they are wet and in the water being fished.

## Hair and Fur

There are many different types of fur. You might use fox, badger, muskrat, beaver, or rabbit fur. Fur is mainly used for dubbing. Dubbing can be any natural fur or manmade material that is cut up or blended, which can be twisted onto the tying thread. It is like making your own yarn that can be wrapped onto the hook to make a fly body. Dubbing can be used to make buggy-looking bodies. Fur can also be used for making wings. To make a wing we mainly use fox, muskrat, or beaver fur.

There are also many types of hair. These include elk, deer, buck tail (the tail

Woodchuck fur. The guard hairs can be used for tails, legs, wings, and antenna.

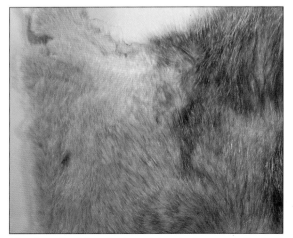

Muskrat fur. The darker, shiny hairs are called guard hairs. They can be used for tails and legs. The soft grey fur is called underfur. Underfur makes really good dubbing for fly bodies.

Different types of fly-tying fur. From left to right: grey fox tail, rabbit fur dyed olive green, red fox tail, arctic fox tail.

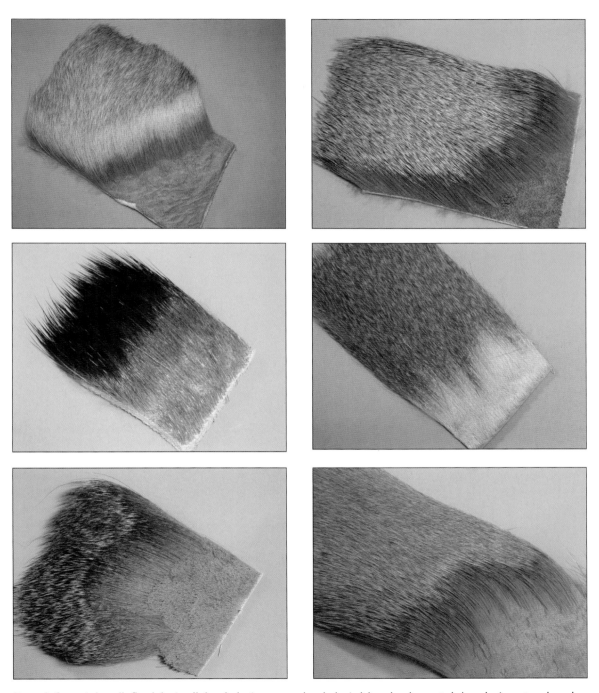

From left to right: elk flank hair, elk body hair, moose body hair, bleached coastal deer hair, natural mule deer hair, dyed mule deer hair. These hairs are used for tails and wings on dry flies because they are stiff and hollow, which make them float very well. Mule deer hair is used to make deer hair bass poppers and divers because it can be tied onto the hook and then trimmed with scissors to make shapes.

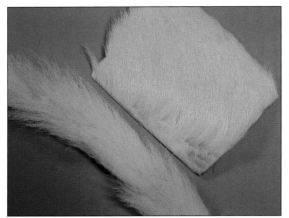

Calf tail and calf body hair are used for tails and wings on dry flies, streamers, and even some saltwater flies.

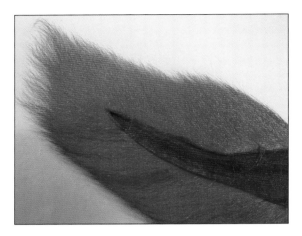

Buck tail dyed red. The top photo is the back side of the buck tail, and the bottom photo is the front side of the buck tail. We will use buck tail to tie a Clouser Minnow (page 121).

of a deer), moose, and antelope hair. These hairs can be used to make wings, too. Deer, elk, and antelope hair can all be used to make hair bodies for minnows and frogs.

## Dubbing

Dubbing can be made of real fur or synthetic (fake or manmade) fur. We most often use dubbing to make a body. We can sometimes make dubbing at home out of hair from the face of a rabbit (hare's mask). You can also buy it pre-made from a fly shop. Some natural dubbing will have sparkly stuff mixed or blended in it. When dubbing is made with synthetics, it is mainly plastic and sparkly stuff all mixed up to look pretty. Dubbing can come in many different colors.

Hare's mask. This fur can be cut off the skin and mixed up to make one of the best natural dubbing materials. Most natural fur makes good dubbing.

This is dry-fly dubbing that comes in a neat dispenser that has 30 different colors. You can tie a lot of different flies in different colors. Dry-fly dubbing is supposed to help your flies float better.

This is squirrel dubbing in a dispenser. There are natural colors and dyed colors. A pre-made dispenser like this is a good way to start out because you have several colors to tie different flies. If you look really close at the dubbing, you will see that there is some synthetic material mixed in with the squirrel fur. This makes it look more lifelike when it is wet.

## Wire, Tinsel, Chenille, and Yarn

Wire is mainly made of copper, but can be made with other materials. We use wire to rib the bodies of flies. Tinsel is mostly made out of metal, but it also can be made out of a plastic called Mylar. It comes in two primary colors—silver and gold. Tinsel can be used to rib a body or to make a body. Chenille is made from artificial dubbing woven on two strings. Chenille can be used to make a body or a tail that will look buggy in the water. Some yarns that you find at an arts and crafts store can be used for tying flies. You can get yarn in many colors. Yarn can be used to make wings, tails, and streamer bodies.

A bunch of different colored copper wire. Wire is used to make bodies on flies that will sink. It can also be wrapped over other body materials to make the fly stronger. This is called ribbing.

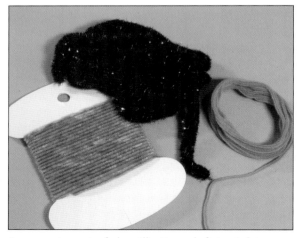

An assortment of chenille. From left to right: regular chenille, Antron sparkle chenille, Ultra chenille. Chenille is used for making fly bodies. We will use Ultra chenille to make a San Juan Worm fly (page 60).

A variety of different tinsel. Tinsel is used to make bodies flash or sparkle. It is also used for ribbing.

## Flashy Stuff

Flashy stuff can be anything that is flashy, like Sparkle Braid, Flashabou, or even tinsel that you can buy right after Christmas when it's on sale because it didn't get bought to decorate someone's house. You can use this flashy stuff to make the body on a fly. You can also use it to make a ribbed body, or to add flash to a tail or wing. Mylar tubing is braided Mylar strips that form a tube and can be used to make a tail, body, wing, or throat on a fly. Some Mylar tubing is sparkly, but there are kinds that aren't sparkly as well.

Sparkle Braid is just one kind of flashy material that can be used to make fly bodies. This could be used on a Woolly Bugger instead of chenille.

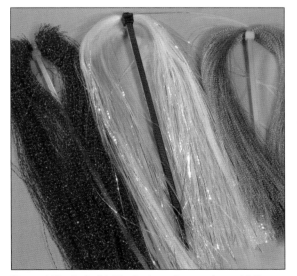

Krystal Flash (left), Flashabou (center), and Micro Krystal Flash (right). These can be used to make tails, wings, bodies, ribbing, or just to add a little accent of flash into the tail or wing of a fly.

Mylar tubing can be used to make bodies, tails, or wings.

## Beads, Cones, and Eyes

Beads are normally made from metal, but can also be made from plastic or glass. The bead is what we put on the front of the hook to make it sink. It also makes the fly look shiny. Some beads are silver, gold, or bronze. Others are orange or red and are meant to imitate a fish egg.

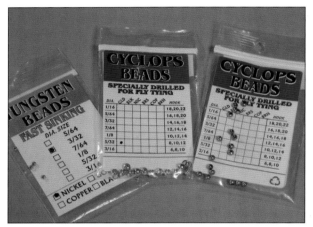

Metal beads used for making bead-head flies. From left to right: tungsten beads, gold beads, olive-colored brass beads.

Metal cone-heads are used on large nymphs and streamers. Here are some red cone-heads and bright green cone-heads.

Cone-heads look a lot like bullets. Like beads, they are put on the front of the hook. A cone-head is supposed to look like the shape of a minnow's head in the water. It can help the fly sink to deeper areas in a lake or help it to sink quickly in a fast-moving stream or river.

Eyes are a fun part of fly tying. Most eyes are made out of plastic, but others, like barbells, are made of metal so they will help the fly sink. Some plastic eyes have a layer of glue on the back of them so they will stick, but for others you'll have to apply your own glue. Barbell eyes have

These are brass barbell eyes in different sizes.

These pre-painted lead eyes are like the brass barbell eyes, but are painted to look like an eye with a pupil. They are very heavy and will make a fly sink really fast.

to be figure-eight wrapped to the hook and you have to post them so your figure-eight wraps don't slip on the hook. Figure-eight wraps are wraps of thread that crisscross over the center of the eyes to hold them to the hook. Posting the figure-eight wraps is done by just wrapping the tying thread around the base of the barbell and the wraps of thread that are created when making the figure-eight wraps. Posting tightens the pressure of the figure-eight wraps so the eyes stay put. I'll show you how to do this later on in the book.

## Rubber Legs, Foam, and Other Fun Stuff

Rubber legs, or silly legs, are one of the most fun materials I've used to tie flies. Silly legs can be used to make a tail or legs, including realistic legs and popper legs. Some foams come with a layer of glue on the back so you can stick two or more layers together. Others don't have any glue at all. Foam can be used to make a popper head and to make a beetle back.

On the left and right are plastic eyes that are not pre-glued. In the middle are holographic stick-on eyes that work really well on streamers to match a baitfish.

These are round rubber legs. They come in bands like this and you just pull them apart. These can be used to make legs on nymphs or grasshopper flies. They come in many different colors.

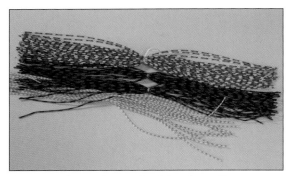

These are barred round rubber legs. They are colored and have small black bars on them to make them look more like bug legs.

These are different colors of closed-cell foam. This floats really well and can be used for a lot of different flies. We'll use some of the green metallic foam when we tie a beetle (see page 132).

Here are different coatings or glues that can be used to color parts of your fly or glue the thread head of your fly so it doesn't come apart. Superglue works well for gluing eyes onto your flies. Remember to always get help from your parents when using these coatings. Superglue can glue your skin together and that can be very dangerous. Always follow the instructions on the container of the coating.

## Keeping It All Organized

Now that we know what some materials are, we can learn how to organize them. One way to organize your materials is to keep them in separate containers and to label the containers. You can get an organizer that has separate compartments for your different hooks to go into. It's always a great idea to label each of the boxes and compartments that you have so you know where all your materials are.

This is a hook organizer that has individual compartments and a magnetic bottom. It's great because if you drop it, the hooks will stay put.

It's always a great idea to label each of the boxes and compartments that you have so you know where all your materials are.

This is a foam fly-tying tool organizer. You can see that there are holes to hold bobbins, scissors, glue, and all your other fly-tying tools so they're easy to get to and keep together. You can make one like this yourself by drilling different size holes in a block of wood.

Some plastic containers have drawers that work really well for storing and organizing hooks and materials on spools, like thread, wire, and tinsel.

As you start to gather more fly-tying materials, it's helpful to keep them organized so you can find what you need, when you need it. Clear plastic boxes with snap-on lids work really well for this. You can write on the end of them with a marker or put a label on them so you know what's in each box.

# Learning the Basics of Fly Tying

Before we jump right in and start tying flies, we need to learn a few basic techniques to get us started off on the right path. Fly tying is all about practicing. The more you practice, the better you'll get and the more fun you'll have.

## Placing a Hook in the Vise

Be careful to only place the bend of the hook into the jaws of the vise. You want the shank to be above the tips of the jaws. This will make it easier to wrap thread and materials on the hook, especially when working near the back of the hook where the bend of the hook begins to curve down from the shank.

When you place the hook in your vise, the hook shank should be parallel to or angled just slightly upward from your tying table or bench. This will help keep materials and thread from sliding forward and falling off the hook.

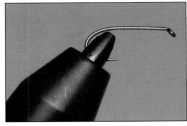
Improper placement of the hook in the jaws of the vise. The hook is set too low in the jaws.

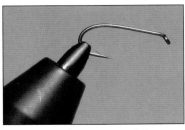
Improper placement of the hook in the jaws of the vise. The shank is pointing downward.

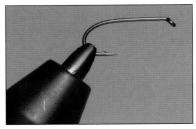
The correct way to place the hook into the jaws of the vise.

## Threading Your Bobbin

There are two ways to thread your bobbin. The first one is to use a bobbin threader, which can be as simple as a bead holding a wire bent in an oval shape. To thread the bobbin, you stick the wire of the bobbin threader through the tube of the bobbin and put the thread through the loop of the wire. Then pull out the bobbin threader and you have a threaded bobbin.

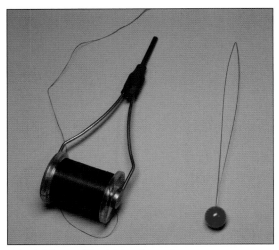
A bobbin and bobbin threader.

The other method is to wet the end of the thread and stick it up the tube of the bobbin. Then suck at the opposite end of the tube, and the thread should suck up out of the bobbin. Pull the rest of the slack thread out and you again have a threaded bobbin.

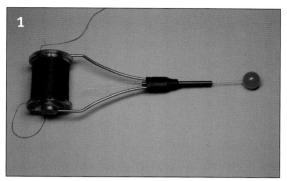

Bobbin with the threader placed inside the tube.

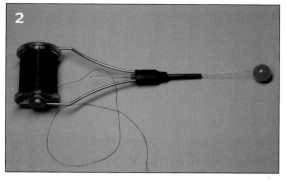

The thread is placed through the loop in the threader.

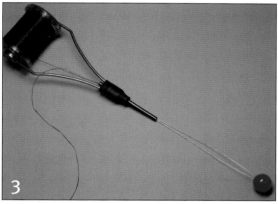

The bobbin threader is pulled back through the bobbin tube. You can see the thread going into the tube.

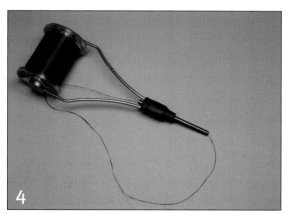

Here's the bobbin completely threaded and ready to wrap thread on a hook.

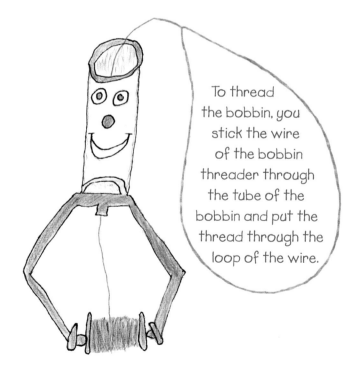

To thread the bobbin, you stick the wire of the bobbin threader through the tube of the bobbin and put the thread through the loop of the wire.

# Starting the Thread on the Hook and Thread Wrapping

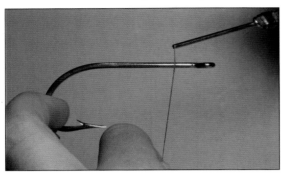

**Step 1:** Start near the eye of the hook. Hold the bobbin in your dominant hand and the tag-end of the thread in your other hand. Place the thread on the side of the hook closest to you, with the bobbin on top of the hook shank. Hold the tag (the short end of the thread) down towards the table.

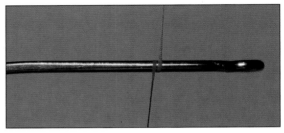

**Step 2:** Use the bobbin to wrap the thread around the shank. Wrap towards the hook's eye. The tag end of thread is held in the same spot and not wrapped.

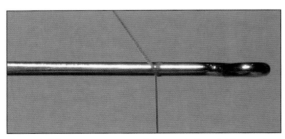

**Step 3:** The next wrap of thread should be going towards the barb end of the hook, so it crosses back over the first wrap of thread and the tag-end.

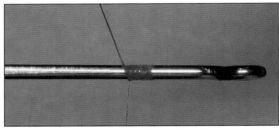

**Step 4:** Continue to wrap toward the back of the hook. Wrap over the tag-end to secure it to the hook shank. Try to make each wrap side-by-side; by doing this you'll make a smooth foundation to wrap the rest of your materials on.

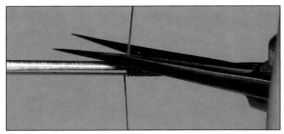

**Step 5:** After you have made six to eight wraps of thread over the tag-end, trim off the tag.

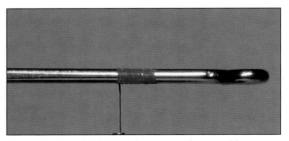

**Step 6:** Good job! You have just learned how to start the thread on the hook. Practice this, because you have to do this on every fly you tie!

# Half Hitch and Whip Finish

The half hitch and the whip finish are two types of knots that we use in fly tying to secure the wraps of thread that make the head on the fly. The first knot, the half hitch, is a simple knot that you can tie with just your fingers. You can use this knot between tying steps to help hold thread wraps and materials in place. You can also finish off your flies with three or four half hitch knots to keep the head of the fly secured.

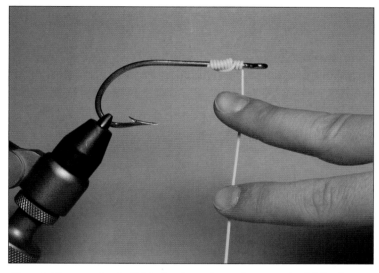

**Step 1:** To start the half hitch, place the pointer and middle fingers of your dominate hand on top of the thread in a V shape. Hold the bobbin in your opposite hand.

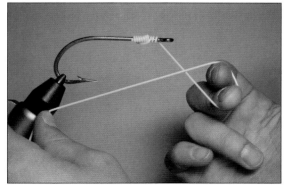

**Step 2:** Wrap the thread from the bobbin over the top of your fingers and rotate your fingers clockwise so the thread crosses over itself. It'll make the shape of a triangle.

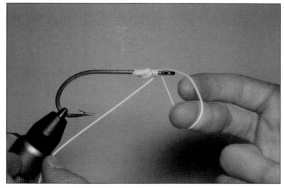

**Step 3:** Put the eye of the hook through the loop of thread.

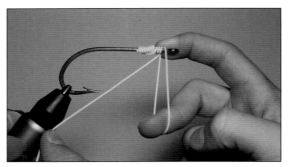

**Step 4:** Take your pointer finger out of the loop and place it against the hook shank and the thread to keep the loop at the spot you want the knot to be tied.

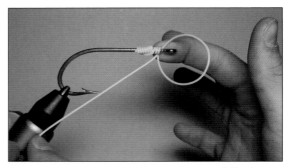

**Step 5:** Now you can remove your middle finger from the loop.

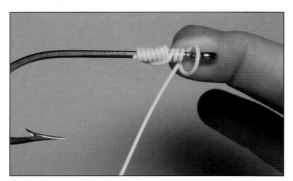

**Step 6:** With your opposite hand, pull on the bobbin so it starts to tighten the loop of thread towards the hook.

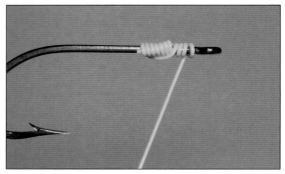

**Step 7:** Finish pulling it tight to complete the half hitch knot.

You can tie a whip finish with just your fingers, but I prefer to use a tool that is made for tying it. I think the whip finish knot is a stronger knot to finish your flies with than the half hitch. There are several types of whip finish tools, but I find the Matterelli brand is the easiest one to use. It comes with good instructions on how to use the tool, but I'll give you a quick lesson anyway. I used fly line for the pictures so it is easy to see the wraps.

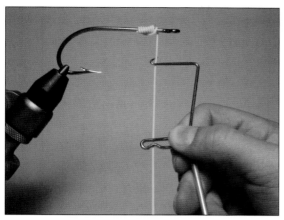

**Step 1:** Place the hook of the tool on the tying thread and bring the thread up into the groove in the bottom arm of the tool.

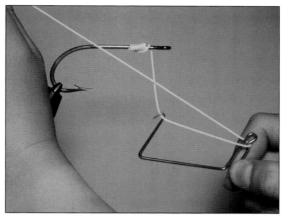

**Step 2:** Let the tool rotate and form kind of a triangle of thread. This is a lot like making the half hitch with your fingers.

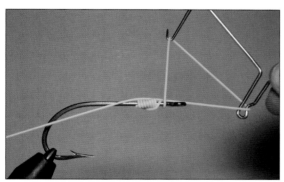

**Step 3:** Next, place the spot where the two threads cross over each other on the side of the fly's head, or in this case, the eye of the hook.

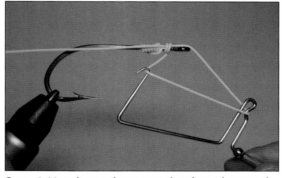

**Step 4:** Use the tool to wrap the thread around the hook. Wrap toward the hook's eye. Usually three to four wraps are plenty for a good whip finish knot.

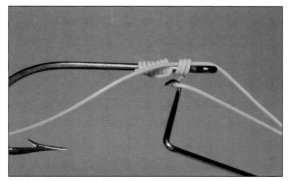

**Step 5:** This is a close-up of the three wraps that will form the knot.

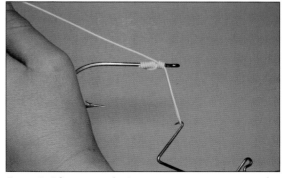

**Step 6:** After completing your wraps, remove the grooved end of the tool from the thread so just the hook of the tool is holding the thread.

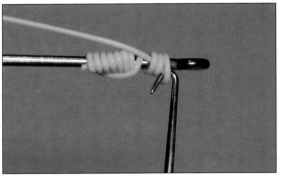

**Step 7:** Pull on the thread from the bobbin until the loop is tight against the head of the fly.

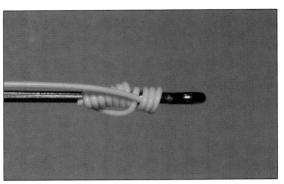

**Step 8:** Remove the hook end of the tool from the thread and finish tightening the knot by pulling on the bobbin.

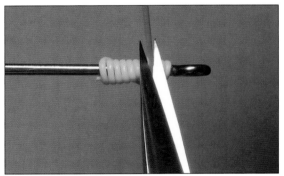

**Step 9:** Once the knot is tight, cut the thread as close as possible to the head of the fly.

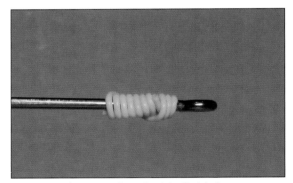

**Step 10:** The completed whip finish knot.

# Tying Materials on the Hook

There are a couple of simple ways to tie materials onto the hook. Different methods work better with different materials. You can experiment and see what works best for you.

Different methods work better with different materials. You can experiment and see what works best for you.

## Pinch Loop Method

The pinch loop method involves pinching a loose loop of thread in your fingertips and then pulling it tight so it grabs the material and secures it to the hook. This method works well for tying on tails or any time you need a material tied directly on top of the hook. I'll use a piece of fly line to represent the materials I am tying onto the hook.

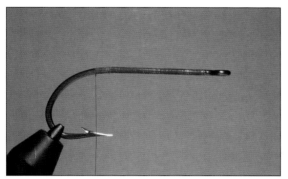

**Step 1:** Begin with the thread at the point you want to tie the material on the hook. In this example we'll pretend we're tying on a tail.

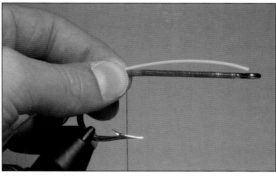

**Step 2:** Hold the material in your fingertips, right at the spot you want to tie the material to the hook.

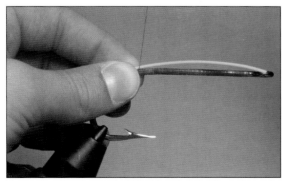

**Step 3:** Lift the bobbin up so the thread is going above the hook shank.

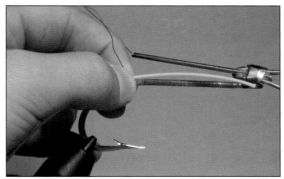

**Step 4:** Then move the thread back into your finger tips and pinch it. A loop of loose thread is formed.

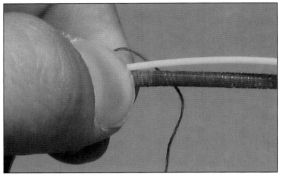

**Step 5:** Bring the bobbin down the backside of the hook shank, but don't let go of the thread pinched in your fingertips.

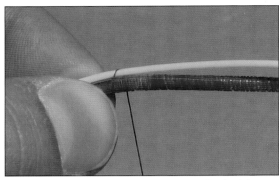

**Step 6:** Now pull straight down on the bobbin, and the loop of thread will pull tight to the material and hook shank. Since the material is in your fingertips, it won't roll over to the opposite side of the hook, but will stay right on top.

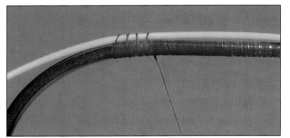

**Step 7:** While keeping tension on the thread, make several wraps over the material to really lock it down tight to the hook.

## Thread Roll Method

The thread roll method uses the tying thread to move or roll the material into place when you're tying it onto the hook. For this method, the material is held against the hook close to where you want it to end up. Let the thread wrap(s) do the work to get it into just the right place. This usually works best with round materials and materials that are hard or stiff because they will roll better. Again, I will use a piece of fly line for my material so it's easy to see and understand.

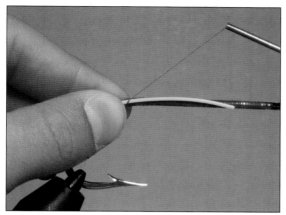

**Step 1:** Let's pretend we want to tie this material on for a tail and it needs to be tied on the top of the hook shank. Start by holding the material parallel with the hook shank on the side of the hook closest to your body. The first wrap of thread needs to wrap over the material with light pressure.

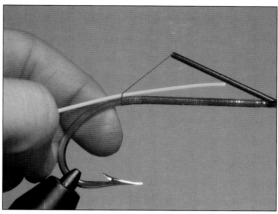

**Step 2:** As the thread goes over the material and more pressure is applied to the thread, the material will roll from the side of the hook to the top of the hook.

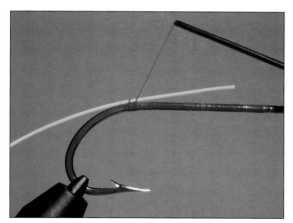

**Step 3:** As you wrap the thread all the way around the hook, you'll want to pull straight up to fully secure the material to the hook. Make sure to keep pressure on the thread until you make several more wraps.

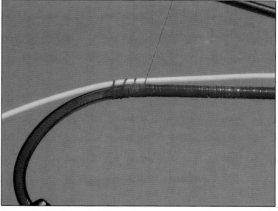

**Step 4:** Make additional wraps over the material while keeping tight thread pressure.

## Soft-Loop Method

The soft-loop method is another way of tying a material to the hook. Basically, the material is held firmly in place and a soft loop of thread is made over it. Once a full wrap has been made around the hook and material, the thread is gradually tightened with even pressure to secure the material. We'll pretend that we're tying a ribbing material on the underside of the hook to demonstrate this method. Again, the fly line represents the material.

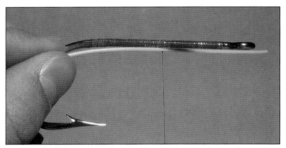

**Step 1:** The tying thread is at the point where the material is to be tied to the hook. The material is placed on the underside of the hook for this demonstration.

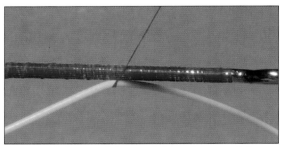

**Step 2:** Make a soft loop of thread around the hook shank and over the material. The thread should be in contact with the shank and material the entire time. If you leave slack in the thread, it will be very difficult to control where the material ends up.

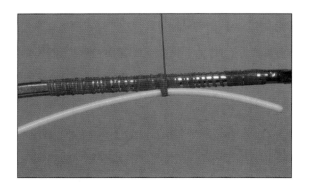

**Step 3:** Once you have made one complete loop around the hook, make your next wrap slightly tighter. You'll always want to tighten the thread in the opposite direction you want the material to be tied in. For example, if you want the material tied in on the underside of the hook, then you will pull the thread tight while lifting upwards away from the hook. Always finish this process by completing a full wrap of thread around the hook and the material being tied in place.

Now that we have learned about hooks, fly-tying tools, materials used for fly tying, and some basic techniques, let's turn the page and learn to tie some flies that we can go catch a fish with!

# 5 Tying Nymphs

## San Juan Worm

The San Juan Worm is one of the most basic flies to tie and to fish with. It's supposed to imitate an aquatic worm that lives in the sand, gravel, and mud on the bottom of rivers

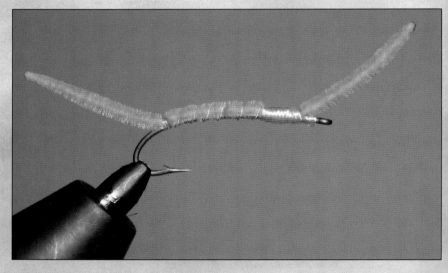

and lakes. I've caught some of my biggest fish on this fly. I even caught a Junior International Game Fish Association (IGFA) World Record fish on this fly pattern. It was a Kokanee salmon that I caught on the East River in Colorado.

The day I caught that salmon, I was fishing with my whole family. We'd been catching fish all day long and my sister had already caught some big Kokanee. I was exploring a new place to fish when I hooked a salmon. It was a very strong fish and it took a while to land. But when I landed him and did all the measuring and weighing, he weighed two pounds and was around twenty inches long! My sister, Ava, also caught a Junior IGFA world record Kokanee salmon that day, and her fish was bigger than mine!

The San Juan Worm is mainly fished in rivers and streams, but at times can be fished in ponds and lakes. When you fish the San Juan Worm in a stream or river, you fish it on the bottom and let it drift downstream. When you fish it in a pond or lake, you can strip it, but you still want it to be on the bottom to make it look like it is in its real habitat.

The San Juan Worm is a fly that lands lots of different fish species. The main fish you catch on a San Juan Worm are trout, bass, salmon, and sunfish. Make sure you read through the directions a couple times before you start tying.

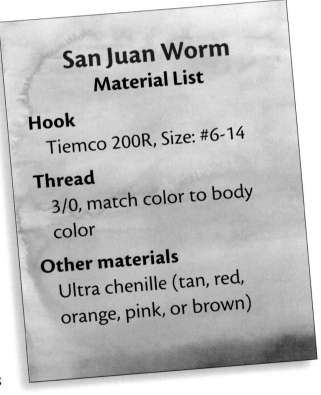

### San Juan Worm
#### Material List

**Hook**
Tiemco 200R, Size: #6-14

**Thread**
3/0, match color to body color

**Other materials**
Ultra chenille (tan, red, orange, pink, or brown)

**Step 1:** Place the hook in the vise.

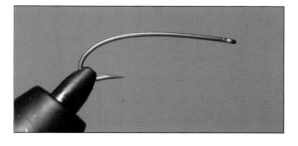

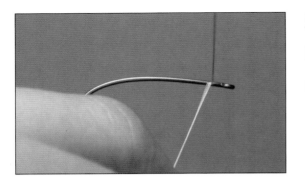

**Step 2:** Start your thread on the hook, and wrap around hook 5 or 6 times.

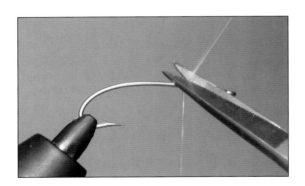

**Step 3:** Cut off the tag end of the thread with your scissors.

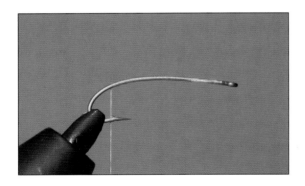

**Step 4:** Wrap the thread toward the back of the hook and stop when your thread is hanging above the barb. (*Note:* I call this place on the hook the starting point.)

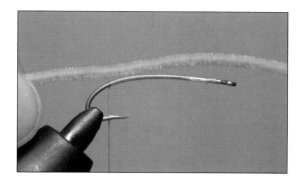

**Step 5:** Cut a piece of ultra chenille that is about two times longer than the hook shank. Hold the chenille so that equal amounts are in front of the hook eye and behind the hook bend.

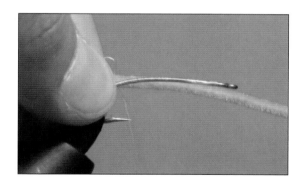

**Step 6:** Hold the chenille right at the starting point and make a pinch-loop.

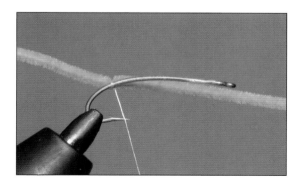

**Step 7:** Pull the pinch-loop tight and make two more tight thread wraps to hold the chenille on top of the hook shank. If it rolls over to the side of the hook, just unwrap your thread and try again.

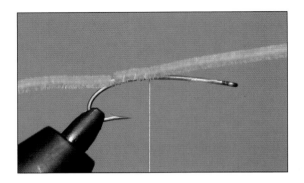

**Step 8:** Wrap your thread toward the hook eye, making sure the thread stays the same distance apart between the wraps. You will probably make about four to eight wraps depending on how big a hook you're using. This will form segments for the body of your worm. To make even wraps, angle your bobbin toward the front of the hook the entire time you wrap and keep the same angle with each turn of the thread.

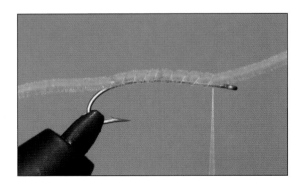

**Step 9:** Continue wrapping forward and stop about one hook-eye length behind the eye. This will leave enough room to make your half-hitch knots or whip-finish knot.

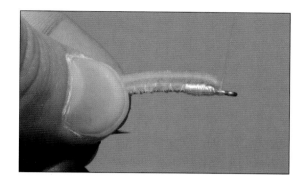

**Step 10:** Next, build up a bump of thread by wrapping back and forth at the front of the body. This will look like the band that a worm has. Then pull the chenille at the front of the body back so you can wrap in front of it with your thread to make a small head.

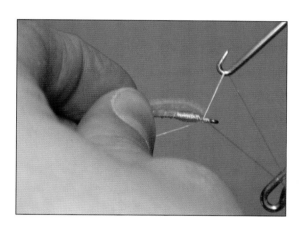

**Step 11:** Using your whip-finish tool, make a good knot to secure the thread. You can use a series of three or four half-hitch knots to finish off the head of your fly if you do not have a whip-finish tool.

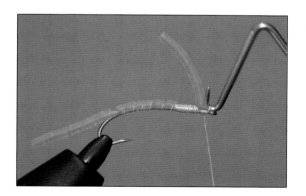

**Step 12:** Complete the whip-finish knot and remove the tool.

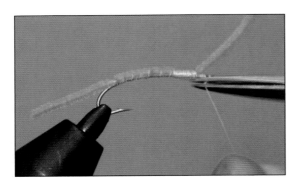

**Step 13:** Trim off the thread with your scissors. Make sure to trim it as close as possible to the head of the fly so there is not a fuzzy tag of thread sticking out.

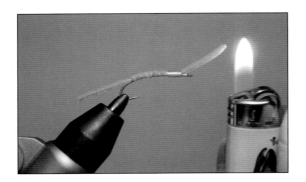

**Step 14:** To make your worm look more realistic, you can just lightly touch a lighter flame to the ends of the chenille. (Note: *Always* have one of your parents or an adult help with this, because the chenille can start on fire very easily.)

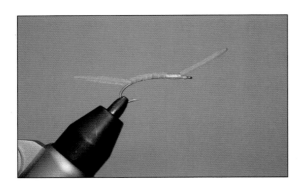

**Step 15:** You have just completed a San Juan Worm. Great Job! Here is a close up view of the finished fly.

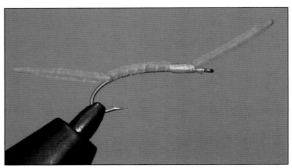

Here is a Kokanee salmon that was caught on an orange San Juan Worm.

# Brassie

The Brassie is a great fly that is fun, quick, and easy to tie. This is one of my favorite flies to tie and fish with because

you catch big fish on it. The biggest rainbow trout I ever caught on the South Plate River was on a Brassie.

That happened two summers ago on a very hot, sunny day. It was an ideal day for fishing. As it got close to noon, my dad saw a very large rainbow trout. He had me fish a Brassie. On my third drift through that area I hooked the trout. It was about 20 inches long and weighed somewhere around 3 pounds!

This fly is fished in rivers, streams, lakes, and ponds. When you fish the Brassie in a river or stream, you fish it close to or on the bottom of the streambed. In lakes and ponds, the Brassie is also fished close to or on the bottom, though sometimes it will

## Brassie
### Material List

**Hook**
Tiemco 3761 or 3769,
Size: #8-22

**Thread**
6/0, black, or match color
to body color

**Other materials**
Ultra wire or copper wire
(chartreuse, olive, red,
copper, brown, or pink);
peacock herl

need to be fished closer to the surface. Since a lake or pond is still water, or dead water, you have to strip or twitch the fly. As well as being fished in a variety of places, the Brassie is used for a variety of fish. Some of the fish you can catch are trout, blue gill, crappie, and salmon.

Like I said, the Brassie is an easy fly to tie and catches lots of fish. It also teaches you some great techniques, like how to wrap a body with wire, and how to wrap fragile materials, like peacock feathers, to make a head. The Brassie can be tied to imitate a bug (when tied the color of a bug) or as an impressionistic fly (if you make it any color that does not imitate a bug). I think that you'll love tying the Brassie nymph.

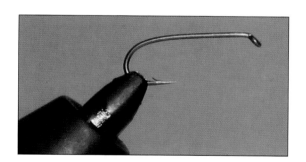

**Step 1:** Place the hook in the vise.

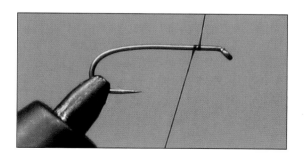

**Step 2:** Start by tying thread on the hook about two hook-eye lengths behind the eye of the hook.

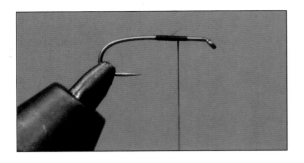

**Step 3:** Once your thread is started, wrap toward the bend of the hook and stop about one-third of the way from the hook eye.

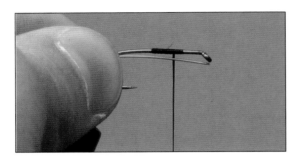

**Step 4:** Place a length of wire under the hook shank where your thread is hanging.

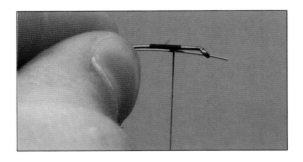

**Step 5:** Use a soft loop of thread to tie the wire to the hook. Make sure to keep it on the underside of the hook.

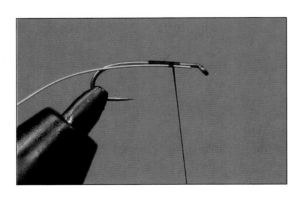

**Step 6:** Once you have made a few wraps of thread, pull the wire toward the bend of the hook and then it'll pull the tip of the wire close to your first thread wraps as it slides under the thread. This keeps you from having to cut the wire with your scissors, which will make the blades dull.

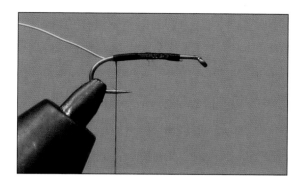

**Step 7:** Continue to wrap over the wire toward the bend of the hook with your thread until you get to the starting point (the spot on the hook shank that's directly above the hook barb).

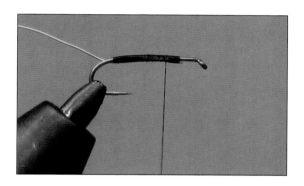

**Step 8:** Wrap your thread forward to the original place that the wire was tied onto the shank (about one third of the way behind the hook eye). This is how far the wire will be wrapped forward to make the body of the fly.

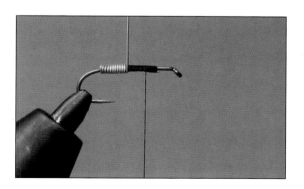

**Step 9:** Begin to wrap the wire forward. Be sure to keep the wraps close together to make a smooth body and to keep the thread from showing between the wraps of wire.

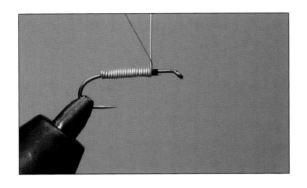

**Step 10:** Stop wrapping the wire when you reach the spot where your thread is hanging. Now hold the wire and cross over it with your thread to tie it to the hook so it won't unwrap.

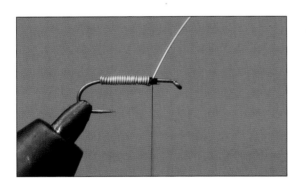

**Step 11:** Make several tight wraps of thread around the wire and the hook so the wire is secure.

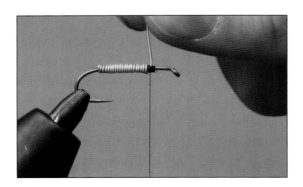

**Step 12:** Hold the wire and rotate it in a circle, keeping pressure away from the hook. The wire will break off right where you wrapped over it with the thread. This keeps you from having to cut it with your scissors.

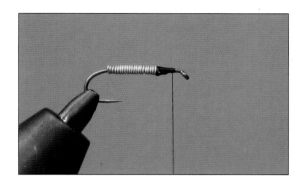

**Step 13:** Make a few more wraps of thread to smooth out the spot where you tied the wire off. The area from the front of the body to the hook eye should be smooth.

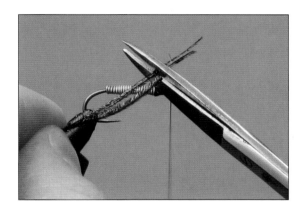

**Step 14:** Select three or four peacock herl strands. Trim their tips even with your scissors.

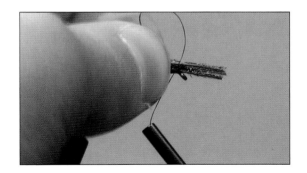

**Step 15:** Hold the peacock herl so the tips go over the hook eye. Form a pinch-loop with your thread. Tighten the loop to secure the herl to the hook.

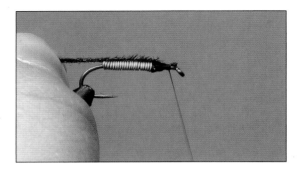

**Step 16:** Make one or two more wraps of thread over the peacock herl. Then pull back on the strands of herl so that they slide under the thread wraps. This is the same technique we used with the wire in step 6. Try not to pull too hard or the strands will break! This keeps you from having to trim the tips of the herl so they do not get tied into the hook eye. If they were to get tied into the hook eye, it would make it very hard to tie your leader to the fly.

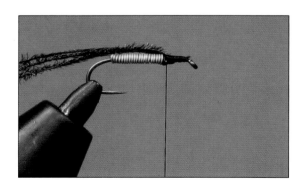

**Step 17:** Make sure you wrap over the strands of peacock herl so they're tied right in front of the wire body.

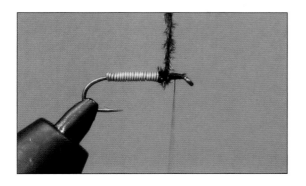

**Step 18:** You can twist the strands of peacock herl so they're like a rope, or they can be wrapped with the strands side-by-side. Then start to wrap them forward from the body towards the hook eye. The herl should be wrapped so they push your tying thread forward as they're wrapped.

**Step 19:** Stop wrapping the herl a short distance behind the hook eye. Be careful not to wrap too far forward or you'll crowd the hook eye with the material.

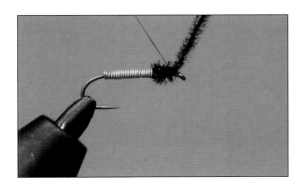

**Step 20:** Hold the strands of peacock herl so you can wrap over them with your tying thread to hold them to the hook so they don't unwind.

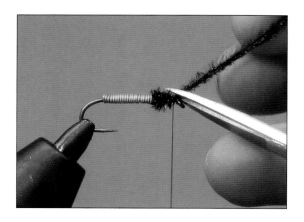

**Step 21:** After you make several tight wraps over the peacock herl, you can trim it off as close to the hook shank as possible. The closer you can cut the herl, the better, but be careful not to cut your thread!

**Step 22:** You can see a few little fuzzy pieces right behind the hook eye. We'll wrap over these with our tying thread to cover them up.

**Step 23:** Make a few wraps of thread so the head of the fly is smooth and all the material has been covered up from the front of the herl to the hook eye.

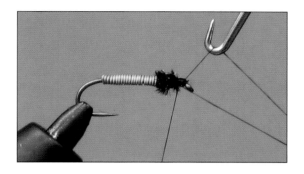

**Step 24:** Make three or four half-hitch knots or use a whip-finish tool to tie off the fly and secure the thread head.

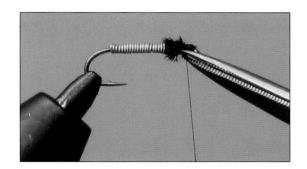

**Step 25:** Trim off the tying thread as close as possible to the head of the fly.

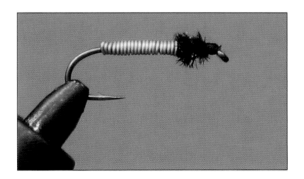

**Step 26:** Congratulations! You have just finished a Brassie.

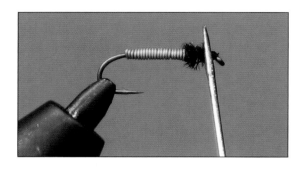

**Step 27:** Head cement can be added to the thread head to help make it more durable.

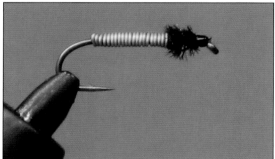

**Step 28:** Here's the finished fly with a nice glossy head. Let's go fishing!

It's done. Let's go fishing!

My sister, Ava, caught this beautiful brown trout on the Gunnison River on a Brassie she tied.

## Soft Hackle Pheasant Tail

The Soft Hackle Pheasant Tail is one of my favorite nymphs to fish because you can strip it, swing it, and twitch it. This fly is a great multi-purpose fly and is also fun to tie. I caught one of my very first green sunfish on it.

One evening, I was fishing with some friends and my dad. The first fly I decided to put on the hook was one I had never used before. It was a Soft Hackle Pheasant Tail. I made my first cast into some weeds because I could see a fish in them. She ate the fly and I was able to land her. The Soft Hackle Pheasant Tail was the hot fly for the rest of the evening! We caught fish almost every cast and they were very big.

This incredible fly can be fished in rivers, streams, ponds, and lakes. In a river or stream, it's best to swing this fly downstream, then twitch it a little when it is directly

### Soft Hackle Pheasant Tail Material List

**Hook**
Tiemco 3761 or 3769,
Size: #10-18

**Thread**
6/0, black or brown

**Other materials**
Ringneck pheasant tail fibers; copper wire; peacock herl or synthetic peacock dubbing; chicken hen neck feather or Hungarian partridge feather

downstream of you. In a lake or pond, you want to let the fly sink for as long as it needs to (depending on how deep the water is), then strip or twitch it.

The Soft Hackle Pheasant Tail can be used on many different fish, including trout, bass, steelhead, salmon, and any kind of panfish. This fly teaches you some great fly-tying techniques. It teaches how to measure a tail, rib a body, dub a thorax, and how to wrap a hackle.

Ever since I first fished the Soft Hackle Pheasant Tail, I've been having fun using and tying it. This is a great fly for a beginner and I think it's a great fly to learn some new techniques from. I hope you enjoy learning how to tie it!

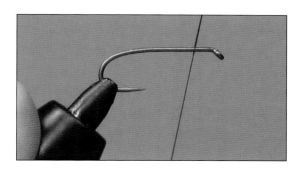

**Step 1:** Place the hook in the vise and start your tying thread on the hook near the hook eye.

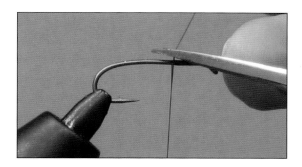

**Step 2:** Trim off the excess tag-end of thread close to the hook shank.

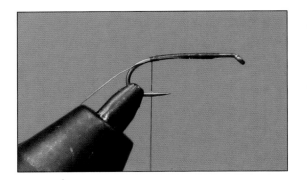

**Step 3:** Tie in copper wire for the ribbing on the underside of the hook shank just like we learned on the Brassie. Wrap over the wire with the tying thread to the back of the hook, or the starting point (the place where the bend of the hook begins to curve away from the hook shank).

**Step 4:** Select six to eight Ringneck pheasant tail fibers that will make the fly tail and body. These can be pulled off the center stem of the tail feather or you can cut them off with your scissors. Be careful to keep the tips of the fibers even for the tail on your fly.

**Step 5:** Hold the pheasant tail fibers with the tips toward the bend of the hook with your fingertips at the hook eye. This is how to measure a material for the tail length you want. On this fly, we will make the tail somewhere between one-half the shank and the full shank length.

**Step 6:** Now that we have the right length measured for our tail, pinch the fibers in your opposite hand and hold them at the starting point to tie them on the hook. Use a pinch-loop to tie them to the hook, making sure the tail stays on the top of the hook and does not spin or roll over to the side. After pulling the pinch-loop tight, make three or four more tight wraps of thread in the same spot to hold the tail.

**Step 7:** Now you can let go of the tail and check to make sure it's the length you wanted and that it's on top of the hook. If it's not right, just unwrap your thread and try again. Remember, there are no rules in fly tying, and you can always do it over to make it just right!

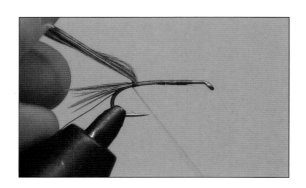

**Step 8:** Pull the long end of the tail fibers back over the tail away from the hook shank so you can wrap the thread in front of them.

**Step 9:** While holding the fibers back out of the way, wrap your thread forward toward the hook eye. Stop your thread about two-thirds of the way up the hook shank. The place you stop your thread will mark the spot your fly body will end after you wrap it.

**Step 10:** Gather the pheasant tail fibers and begin to wrap them forward to form the body. The fibers will break kind of easy if you hit the sharp hook point or pull on them too hard. Don't worry if they break, it happens to everyone. Just back up and try it again.

**Step 11:** Once you've wrapped the pheasant fibers to the spot your thread is hanging, cross over the fibers with the tying thread to secure them to the hook shank. Make several tight wraps to make sure they stay put. You could put a half-hitch knot here to make extra sure they will not unwind.

**Step 12:** Here's the completed body with the pheasant fibers secured to the hook.

**Step 13:** Trim off the excess pheasant fibers with your scissors as close as possible to the hook shank.

**Step 14:** Wrap the copper wire ribbing material over the body in a spiral. The spaces between the wraps should be equal as you wrap the wire forward. This makes the body look segmented like a real bug and makes the pheasant-tail body very strong.

**Step 15:** When you reach the front of the body with the wire ribbing, you'll want to cross over the wire with your tying thread to secure it. This is the same technique we learned when we made the Brassie.

**Step 16:** After several tight wraps of thread over the wire, you can pull on the wire while rotating it in a circle and it'll break off close to the hook shank.

**Step 17:** Take a small amount of the peacock synthetic dubbing and pull it apart so it's fluffy. If it's stuck together, it won't twist onto the thread very easily.

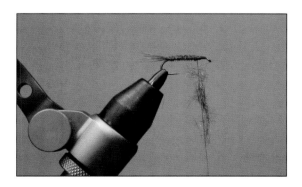

**Step 18:** Lightly lay the dubbing on the tying thread. The wax on the thread is a little sticky and will help to hold it there.

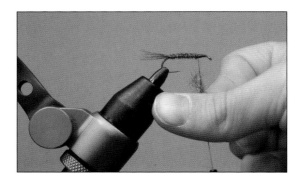

**Step 19:** To make the dubbing stick to the thread so it can be wrapped on the hook, use your thumb and pointer finger to roll it on the thread tightly. Dubbing takes practice and you'll learn that different dubbing materials take more or less pressure with your fingers to make it stick. See the next step before you start to roll the dubbing.

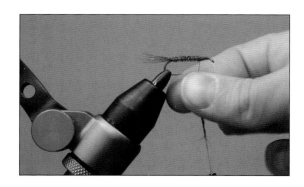

**Step 20:** It's very important to stay on one spot at a time when you roll the dubbing and thread between your finger and thumb. Pinch the thread and dubbing and squeeze the two together while you roll your fingers. Also, only roll one direction *not* back and forth. Usually if you roll back and forth, the dubbing won't stick to the thread.

**Step 21:** Once the dubbing is rolled tightly onto the thread, you're ready to wrap it on the hook to make the thorax (the front part of the body). Most new fly tiers like to use too much dubbing. I still do that sometimes. You only need enough to change the color of your thread.

**Step 22:** This is a close-up of the dubbing material ready to be wrapped.

**Step 23:** Wrap the dubbing around the hook to make the thorax. The thorax should start right in front of the body.

**Step 24:** Select a small Hungarian partridge body feather or a chicken hen neck feather for the soft hackle on this fly. A partridge feather is pictured.

**Step 25:** Next, pull off the fluffy stuff that is on each side of the stem on the bottom of the feather.

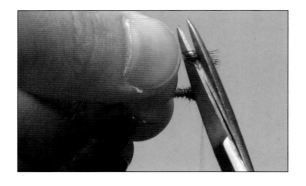

**Step 26:** Hold the feather by the tip and fold the fibers on each side of the feather away from the tip so you can trim it. This will be the spot where we tie the feather onto the hook.

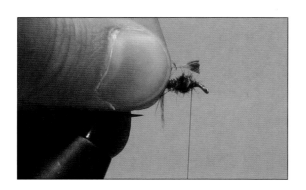

**Step 27:** This shows the fibers folded back and held in your fingers. The tip has been clipped off. The small triangle is what you're going to tie to the hook. It'll go right in front of the dubbed thorax.

**Step 28:** Tie the feather to the hook with several tight wraps. A soft-loop is a good way to catch the tip of the feather. Then make a few more secure wraps. (*Note:* The curve of the feather should be curving down towards the tabletop. If it's tied this way, it'll make the hackle fibers point back over the body because of their natural curve.)

**Step 29:** Hold the stem of the feather with hackle pliers or your fingers and start to wrap it around the hook in front of the dubbing.

**Step 30:** Finish wrapping the hackle feather forward toward the hook eye. Once you have enough hackle on the hook (two or three turns), cross over the stem of the feather with the tying thread and make three or four tight wraps to secure it. Make sure to leave room to make a head and whip-finish your fly. If you crowd the hook eye with material, it will be very hard to put your leader though the eye when you try to fish it.

**Step 31:** Trim off the hackle feather stem as close as possible to the point it was tied off with the thread.

**Step 32:** Here you can see how close the stem is trimmed. If it's trimmed close it will be easy to make a nice head on the fly.

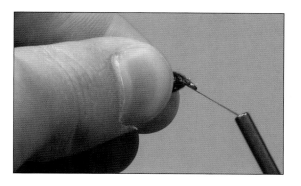

**Step 33:** Gently pull the hackle fibers back over the body and hold them while you make wraps to cover up the stem of the feather and make a head on the fly.

**Step 34:** Get the whip-finish tool ready to complete the fly.

**Step 35:** Whip-finish, remove the tool and pull the knot tight. Be careful not to wrap into the hackle when you are whip-finishing the fly.

**Step 36:** Clip off the tying thread really close to the head. You can put some head cement on the head now.

**Step 37:** The finished Soft Hackle Pheasant Tail. Wow, you did a great job! Keep on practicing so you get even better at tying flies.

I like to fish Soft Hackle Pheasant Tails because they catch a lot of fish, and some are pretty big ones!

# 6 Tying Streamers

## Woolly Bugger

I remember as a little boy tying my first fly, a Woolly Bugger. I sat on my dad's lap and he held his hand over mine on the bobbin and helped me make wraps on the hook. The Woolly Bugger is also one of the first flies I

ever fished, and it's the fly that I caught my first fish on.

Even though I was really young (it was one day before my third birthday), I still remember catching that first fish. My dad and I were fishing on the Uncompahgre River in Colorado. It was getting close to the end of the day when I hooked a fish. It was a brown trout about 18 inches long. I cast to it, hooked it, landed it, and released it all on my own. It was unbelievable to catch a fish on a fly I tied!

This type of fly is called a streamer and is supposed to imitate a minnow or leech. The Woolly Bugger can be fished in ponds, lakes, rivers, and streams. In a pond or a lake, it's mainly stripped and twitched to imitate a minnow. It can also be swung in a river to imitate a minnow or a type of large bug that's floating down the river. You can fish lots of different fish with a Woolly Bugger. Some of these are trout, bass, northern pike, and salmon.

This fly teaches you some great techniques, like how to measure a tail, how to palmer a hackle, how to make a chenille body, and how to rib a body. The Woolly Bugger is one of my favorite flies, and it's an easy fly for beginners to tie. I still use it to this very day and have lots of fun fishing it for all sorts of fish and in different places.

## Woolly Bugger
### Material List

**Hook**
Tiemco 9395, Size: #2-10

**Thread**
3/0, match color to body color

**Other materials**
Marabou feather; copper wire; chenille or sparkle chenille; Estaz, peacock herl, or dubbing; rooster saddle hackle feather

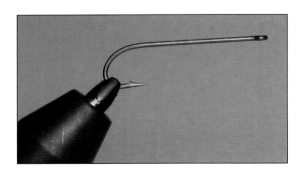

**Step 1:** Place the hook in the vise. Make sure it's secure. Usually streamer hooks are larger than nymph hooks or dry-fly hooks, and it takes a little more pressure to hold them tight.

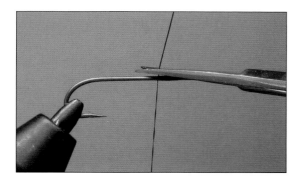

**Step 2:** Start your thread near the hook eye with several wraps of thread. Then trim off the excess tag end of thread.

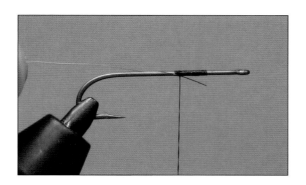

**Step 3:** Tie in a length of copper wire near where you started the thread on the hook. Use the same method as we used on the Brassie to tie the wire. The wire will be the ribbing for our Woolly Bugger and will also hold the hackle feather to the body of the fly.

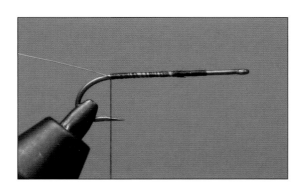

**Step 4:** Wrap over the copper wire toward the bend of the hook to the starting point. This is the spot on the hook where the bend of the hook curves down away from the shank.

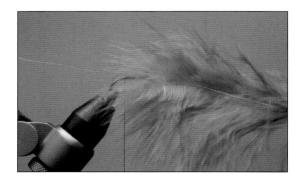

**Step 5:** Select a marabou feather for the tail. We'll pull off a little bit of the fluffy stuff on the bottom of the feather so it's easier to work with while tying the feather for the tail.

**Step 6:** Bunch the marabou fibers together and hold them along the hook shank to measure how long you want the tail of the fly to be. Usually I make Woolly Bugger tails about the same length as the hook shank. You can experiment and make some shorter and some longer. A longer tail will wiggle and jiggle in the water because the marabou's so soft.

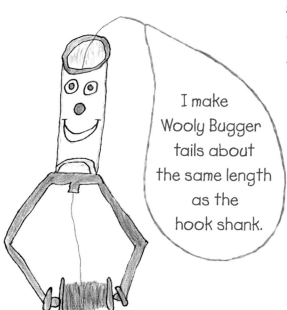

I make Wooly Bugger tails about the same length as the hook shank.

**Step 7:** Once you measure the tail, move it to the back of the hook to the starting point and use the pinch-loop method to tie it in place. Remember to hold onto the tail until you make several tight wraps of thread. This will keep the tail from rolling over to the backside of the hook shank.

**Step 8:** If the tail's the length you want, wrap the thread over the marabou feather toward the hook eye. Make sure not to wrap too far forward and crowd the hook eye. I like to stop about two hook-eye lengths behind the eye.

**Step 9:** Trim off the excess marabou feather close to the hook shank where it was tied down.

**Step 10:** Here's the completed tail for your fly.

**Step 11:** Now wrap over the marabou feather on the hook shank to really tie it down and make a smooth thread underbody to wrap the chenille body of the fly over.

**Step 12:** Chenille is a fuzzy yarn material that has a thread center. We want to cut a length of chenille about six inches long to make our body. For small Woolly Buggers, you'll use less, and for large ones you might use more.

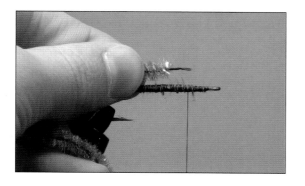

**Step 13:** You can pull the fuzzy stuff away from the thread core on one end of the chenille, like in the picture.

**Step 14:** Using the tying thread, tie the thread core of the chenille to the hook where you trimmed off the marabou feather.

**Step 15:** With the tying thread, wrap back over the chenille all the way down the hook to where the tail is tied. Then wrap the thread forward to where the chenille was tied in by the hook eye. The thread has to be there to tie off the chenille after it has been wrapped to make the body of the fly.

**Step 16:** Begin to wrap the chenille forward to make the body. The first wrap should be right in front of the tail. Each wrap should be right in front of the wrap before it so the body turns out even and smooth.

**Step 17:** Stop wrapping the body where your thread is. Make sure not to get too close to the hook eye with the chenille. Cross over the chenille with the thread and make several tight wraps to hold it in place.

**Step 18:** Trim off the excess chenille with your scissors, close to the hook shank.

**Step 19:** Here's the completed tail and body. You can tie a half-hitch to make sure things don't unwind.

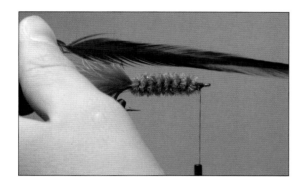

**Step 20:** Select a rooster saddle feather for the hackle feather that we will wrap over the body. There are small packages of these feathers available just for making Woolly Bugger hackles.

**Step 21:** Trim off the fluffy stuff on the bottom of the feather and pull a few fibers off each side of the feather where you cut it. This will leave the stem for you to tie to the hook.

**Step 22:** Tie the feather on the hook right in front of the body. I like to tie it on my side of the hook shank with the shiny side of the feather looking at me. This means the curve is going away from me.

**Step 23:** Start to wrap the feather over the body. The first wrap should be right in front of the body, and then each wrap should be the same distance apart from each other as you wrap back towards the tail. You can hold the feather in your fingers or use hackle pliers.

**Step 24:** Stop wrapping when you get back to the tail.

**Step 25:** Hold the feather so it does not unwind and cross the copper wire over the tip of the hackle feather to hold it to the hook.

**Step 26:** Keep wrapping the copper wire forward through the hackle to secure it to the body.

**Step 27:** Stop wrapping the wire when you get to the front of the body. Cross over the wire with the tying thread and make several tight wraps to hold it in place.

**Step 28:** Pull on the wire and rotate it in a circle so it will break off where it was tied down to the hook. Then make some more thread wraps to form the head of the fly.

**Step 29:** Make a whip-finish knot to complete the fly.

**Step 30:** Trim off the thread with your scissors.

**Step 31:** Remember to trim off the tip of the hackle feather, back by the tail of the fly.

**Step 32:** Here's the finished Woolly Bugger. Watch out fish, here we come!

This brown trout sure liked this Woolly Bugger. This one is tied with a metal cone on the front to help it sink faster.

## Soft Hackle Streamer

The first time I tied the Soft Hackle Streamer was in a fly-tying class taught by a friend of mine named Jack Gartside. This fly is a very fun fly to tie because you tie it on a big hook and you use colorful feathers. This fly will attract lots of fish, and I've caught my biggest bass with it.

I caught that fish at a small farm pond that I was fishing with my dad and a friend of mine. I was fishing next to a weed bed and had been catching some smaller bass that morning. Just as the sun was coming up, I hooked a very large one. It was twenty-two inches long and weighed four pounds!

The Soft Hackle Streamer can be fished in ponds, lakes, streams, and rivers. When you fish it in ponds and lakes, you twitch, strip, and wiggle it to make it look like a bait fish. When you fish it in a river or stream, first cast it across the water to the opposite bank, then swing the fly until it is directly downstream from you, and then twitch it. The Soft Hackle Streamer can also be stripped and pumped.

The Soft Hackle Streamer can be used to catch many different kinds of fish all around the world. I've even fished this fly in Tokyo Bay, Japan, for Japanese sea bass. Some of the fish that can be caught on the Soft Hackle Streamer are bass, trout, northern pike, lake trout, and salmon.

## Soft Hackle Streamer
### Material List

**Hook**
Tiemco 9395 or Tiemco 811s (for saltwater use)

**Thread**
3/0, match color to hackle and wing color

**Other materials**
Tinsel or Sparkle Braid; a few strands of Flashabou or Krystal Flash; marabou feather(s); natural or dyed mallard flank feather; Eyes are optional, and can be glued on to the side of the head when the fly is finished

This fly teaches you the technique of wrapping a marabou feather to make a body and wing that will look like a fish's body when wet. The Soft Hackle Streamer is one of my favorite flies and I highly recommend it for beginners.

**Step 1:** Place the hook in the vise.

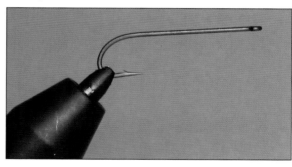

**Step 2:** Start the tying thread near the hook eye.

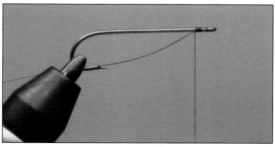

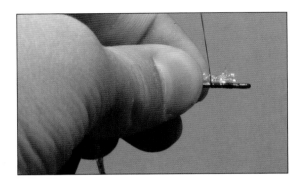

**Step 3:** Trim off the excess tag-end of the thread and cut a piece of Sparkle Braid material about 8 inches long for the body of the fly. Hold the end of the Sparkle Braid close to the hook eye and use the pinch-loop method to tie it on top of the hook.

**Step 4:** Start to wrap the thread over the Sparkle Braid toward the bend of the hook. If you hold the Sparkle Braid up and away from the hook shank as you wrap it down, it will stay on the top of the hook shank.

**Step 5:** Wrap over the Sparkle Braid until it is tied in at the starting point.

**Step 6:** Wrap the tying thread forward toward the hook eye and stop about three hook-eye lengths behind the eye.

**Step 7:** Wrap the Sparkle Braid forward to make the body. Stop when you reach the tying thread, cross over the Sparkle Braid with the tying thread, and make several tight wraps to secure it to the hook.

**Step 8:** Trim off the excess body material close to the hook shank.

**Step 9:** Here's the finished body!

**Step 10:** Pick out one marabou feather (yellow is pictured). Pull all the really fluffy stuff off the bottom of the quill so it looks like the feather in the picture.

**Step 11:** Pick out another marabou feather. It can be the same color as the first one or a different color (white is pictured). Pull off the really fluffy stuff at the bottom of this one too.

**Step 12:** Hold the two feathers with the tips even and the long fluffy fibers folded down away from the tips. Sometimes a little spit on your fingers makes it easier to fold the fibers down.

**Step 13:** Trim off the tip of the feather leaving a small amount of the tip to tie to the hook.

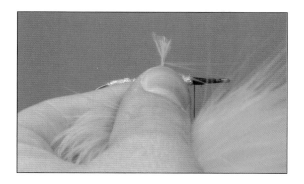

**Step 14:** There should be a small triangle left that will get tied to the hook in front of the body.

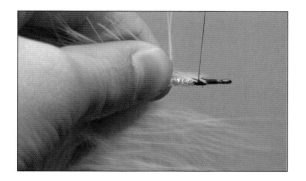

**Step 15:** Hold the long fibers out of the way when you tie the tips of the two feathers to the hook. The soft-loop method is a good way to tie these onto the hook.

**Step 16:** Make several tight wraps to secure the two feathers. Now they are tied on and ready to wrap.

**Step 17:** Hold both feathers together and begin to wrap them to form a soft hackle, or collar. The first wrap should be right in front of the body. Wrap the feathers toward the hook eye with each wrap directly in front of the previous wrap.

**Step 18:** As you wrap the feathers over the top of the hook shank, hold the long, fluffy fibers back out of the way so that you don't wrap over them.

**Step 19:** Keep wrapping forward and stop a short distance behind the hook eye. Then cross over the feathers with the tying thread. Make several tight wraps to hold them in place.

**Step 20:** Trim off the excess feather material close to the hook shank.

**Step 21:** Hold the marabou hackle out of the way and make a few wraps to cover up the spot where the feathers were cut off.

**Step 22:** A couple pieces of Flashabou can be folded around the thread and then tied down on top of the hook shank in front of the marabou hackle.

**Step 23:** You can see the Flashabou is in place on top of the marabou.

**Step 24:** A mallard duck flank feather is used for the front hackle.

**Step 25:** Trim the tip of this feather just like you did the marabou feathers. On this mallard feather, I pulled the fibers off one side of the feather so it would make less hackle as it was wrapped.

**Step 26:** I like to tie the mallard feather in on my side of the hook.

**Step 27:** Begin to wrap the mallard feather around the hook shank. Start right in front of the marabou hackle.

**Step 28:** Wrap the mallard feather around the shank several times. You can experiment with more or less wraps and decide what looks best to you. Cross over the feather with the tying thread and make a couple of tight wraps to hold it in place.

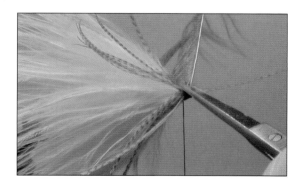

**Step 29:** Trim off the excess mallard feather close to the spot it was tied down with the thread.

**Step 30:** Pull the marabou hackle and the mallard collar back over the hook and hold them there while you build a head on the fly with the tying thread.

**Step 31:** Here, the smooth head is completed.

**Step 32:** Whip finish the fly to secure the thread at the head of the fly.

**Step 33:** Trim off the tying thread as close as possible to the head of the fly.

**Step 34:** Hold the Flashabou back over the hook and trim it off so it's a little longer than the tip of the marabou hackle. If you want to glue eyes on, you can do that now on the sides of the head.

**Step 35:** That was a lot of work, but the fly is finished! I put some water on this one to wet the marabou hackle back so you can see how it has a shape that looks like a small fish.

A Soft Hackle Streamer was responsible for catching this healthy brown trout. Brown trout love streamers of all kinds!

## Clouser Minnow

The Clouser Minnow was created by a man named Bob Clouser. This fly is very simple to tie and is a great fly to fish with. When I went to St. Louis, I fished this fly

in some ponds at the August A. Busch Memorial Conservation Area and caught some really big bass.

That day, I was fishing a Clouser Minnow with a white belly and a green back. I caught a few smaller fish, and then hooked a huge bass. It weighed around four pounds and was about twenty inches long. Later in the day, I caught another bass about the same size!

When you fish the Clouser Minnow, you strip it and then pause for just a second because it does a diving action like some bait fish do. This fly is mostly fished in lakes and ponds, but at times can be fished in a river that is moving slowly. If you fish it in slow water or still water, it will have good diving action. Fast-moving water just sweeps it away, and it won't have a good effect on the action. You can use the Clouser Minnow for many different

### Clouser Minnow
**Material List**

**Hook**
Tiemco 9395 or Tiemco 811S (for saltwater use)

**Thread**
3/0, match color to wing color

**Other materials**
Dumbbell eyes (can be brass or lead); tinsel, Flashabou or Sparkle Braid; buck tail, both light and dark colored

fish in both saltwater and freshwater. In freshwater, you can catch bass, pike, trout, and carp. In saltwater, you can catch sea bass, mackerel, bonefish, tarpon, and redfish.

This fly teaches you some great techniques, like how to tie a hair-wing streamer that will fish upside down, making it more snag-proof. You'll also learn how to make a flash body and how to figure-eight and post a pair of lead eyes to the hook. This is a fun fly to tie and fish because it's quick and easy and works for so many different kinds of fish.

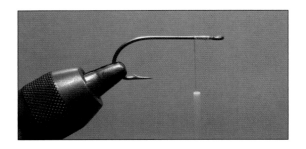

**Step 1:** Place the hook securely in the vise and start the tying thread on the hook near the eye.

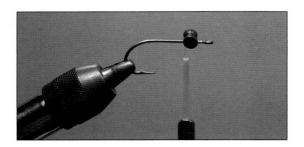

**Step 2:** Attach the dumbbell eyes by figure-eight wrapping (crisscrossing through the middle of the eyes) over them to secure them onto the hook shank. The eyes should be tied about two to three hook-eye lengths behind the eye. It is a good idea to apply a drop of head cement to your thread wraps to help keep the eyes from rotating around the hook on the finished fly.

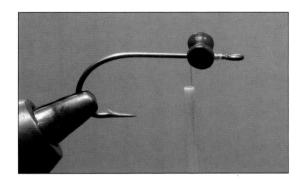

**Step 3:** Here is a close-up view of the mounted dumbbell eyes on the hook.

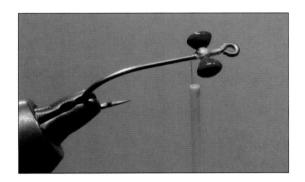

**Step 4:** This is a close-up view of the figure-eight wraps that secure the eyes to the hook.

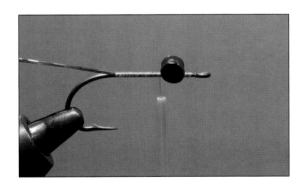

**Step 5:** Tie on the body material (I used Flashabou on this fly) right behind the eyes. Once the body material is tied, wrap over the material to the spot on the shank that is right above the hook point. Next, wrap your thread forward so it's directly behind the dumbbell eyes.

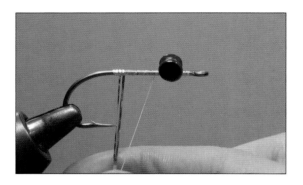

**Step 6:** Begin wrapping the body material forward toward your tying thread.

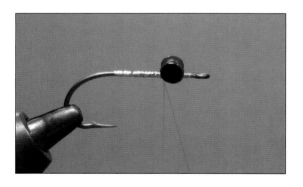

**Step 7:** Wrap forward to the tying thread. Cross your thread over the material to secure it. Make several tight wraps to make sure the material stays in place.

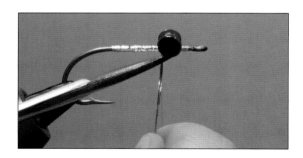

**Step 8:** Trim off the excess body material close the hook shank.

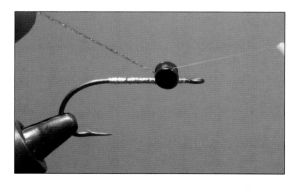

**Step 9:** Fold a couple of strands of Krystal Flash in half and loop them around the tying thread. Position them on the top of the hook shank right behind the eyes.

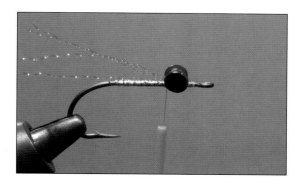

**Step 10:** Make several wraps of thread over the Krystal Flash to hold it in place right behind the eyes.

**Step 11:** Take a small amount of buck tail (white buck tail is pictured) and measure out about two hook lengths to make the underwing, or the bottom, of the finished fly. The length of the buck tail can be longer or shorter to look like different small fish.

**Step 12:** Hold the center of the buck tail right behind the eyes and use a pinch-loop to attach it to the hook. Make several tight wraps once the pinch-loop has been tightened.

**Step 13:** Close-up view of the buck tail tied on the hook behind the eyes.

**Step 14:** Pull the buck tail over the middle of the eyes and hold it while you cross the thread over it to tie it down to the hook shank in front of the eyes.

**Step 15:** Here is a close-up view of the buck tail secured in front of the eyes.

**Step 16:** Cut off the end of the buck tail that is in front of the eyes. Cut close to the hook shank. Make a few thread wraps to cover up the trimmed ends of the hair.

**Step 17:** Turn the hook upside-down in the vice.

**Step 18:** It is a good idea to put some head cement on the thread wraps before tying on the buck-tail wing. This will help glue the wing to the thread and hook shank.

**Step 19:** Take another bunch of buck tail (chartreuse green is pictured) to make the wing. This will go on the opposite side of the hook from the other piece of buck tail. Measure it out so it's the same length as the first piece.

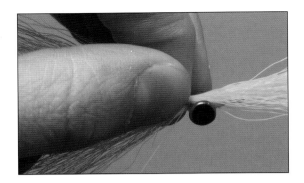

**Step 20:** Use a pinch-loop and several tight wraps of thread to hold the buck tail wing in place behind the eyes.

**Step 21:** Pull the buck tail through the middle of the eyes and secure it in front of the eyes with several tight wraps of thread.

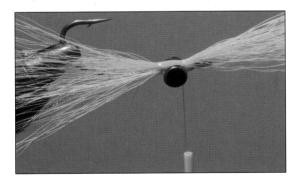

**Step 22:** Here's a close up view of the buck tail secured in front of the eyes.

**Step 23:** Trim off the ends of the buck tail that are in front of the eyes. Make sure you trim close to the thread wraps.

**Step 24:** Make sure to keep the cut ends from going into the hook eye. If they do, it'll make it hard to put your leader through the eye when you fish the fly.

**Step 25:** Wrap thread to cover up the cut ends of the buck tail and form a smooth head on the fly.

**Step 26:** Whip finish to secure the head wraps and complete the fly.

**Step 27:** Cut the thread off close to the head. It's a good idea to put some head cement on the thread wraps to make the fly more durable.

**Step 28:** The finished Clouser Minnow! This will swim with the hook point up so it does not snag on the bottom as easily.

There are a lot of saltwater fish, like this spotted bay bass, that eat the Clouser Minnow. I love this fly because it works so well to catch good fish.

# 7 Tying Dry Flies

## Tyler's Beetle

I started tying my beetle so I could fish for green sunfish at a lake twenty minutes from my home, but I've been using it to catch other fish lately, in-

cluding bass, trout, bluegill, and carp. One of the first fish I caught on a Tyler's Beetle was actually a carp.

I caught that carp at Switzer Lake, the lake near my house. I had been fishing nymphs all morning and catching lots of fish on them. Then I saw some fish rising and decided to put on a dry fly. I chose my beetle pattern. After a few casts, I hooked up with a nice fish. At first I thought it was a bass because it looked and felt much larger than the green sunfish I had been catching most of the morning, but when I pulled it in, I saw it was a carp. It measured about twenty-four inches long and weighed around two pounds.

Tyler's Beetle can be fished in ponds, lakes, rivers, and streams. When you fish any beetle pattern in a lake or pond, you can either let the fly sit stationary in the water or strip it slowly so it looks like it is swimming. When you fish it in a stream or river, you want to cast the fly upstream of you and let it swing downstream with a non-drag drift. I love to fish this beetle for big trout and bass in the summertime.

## Tyler's Beetle
### Material List

**Hook**
Tiemco 100 or Tiemco 9300

**Thread**
6/0, match color to body/shell back

**Other materials**
Tying thread, metallic foam, barred round rubber legs

The Tyler's Beetle teaches you some great techniques, like how to tie in a set of rubber legs and how to make a foam back. This fly is a fun fly to tie and is a great fly to fish. I hope you like this fly and have fun with it!

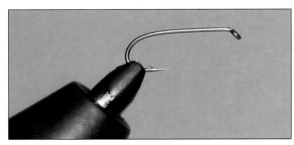

**Step 1:** Place the hook in the vise.

**Step 2:** Start the tying thread near the hook eye.

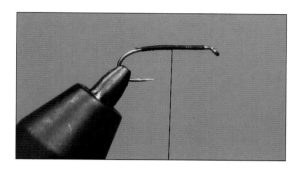

**Step 3:** Wrap the thread down the hook shank to the starting point and then forward so it's right in the middle of the hook shank.

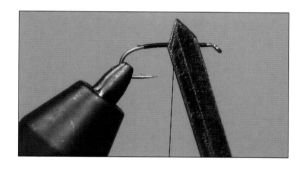

**Step 4:** Cut a strip of closed cell foam about the same width as the gap of the hook. On one end, trim it so it comes to a point in the middle.

**Step 5:** Hold the foam strip on the top of the hook shank with the point where the thread's hanging. If you're using metallic foam like in the picture, the metallic side should be tied down against the shank of the hook. Use the soft-loop method to tie the pointed end of the foam onto the hook.

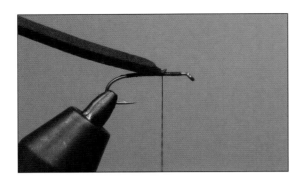

**Step 6:** A close-up view of the point of the foam tied to the hook with several wraps of thread.

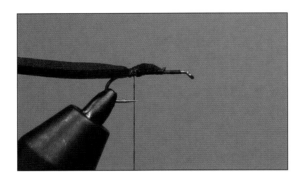

**Step 7:** Wrap the thread back over the foam strip to the starting point.

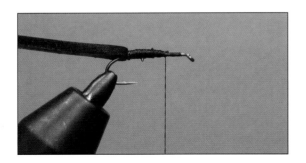

**Step 8:** Now wrap the tying thread forward so it's slightly in front of the middle of the hook.

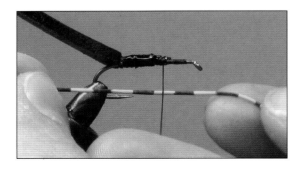

**Step 9:** Apply some head cement to the thread body to make it more durable. Use a short piece of barred round rubber leg material and fold it over the tying thread.

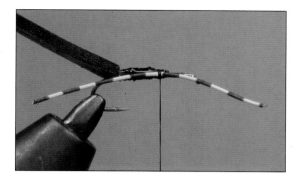

**Step 10:** Slide the barred round rubber leg material up to the side of the hook shank and make a couple of thread wraps over it to hold it in place on the side of the hook. This makes the two legs on your side of the hook.

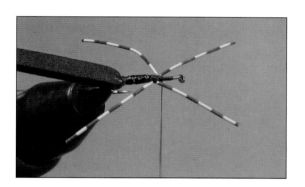

**Step 11:** Repeat this step, making the next set of legs on side of the hook facing away from you.

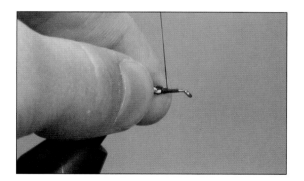

**Step 12:** Hold the front legs back over the hook shank and wrap the tying thread forward so it's in front of the rubber legs.

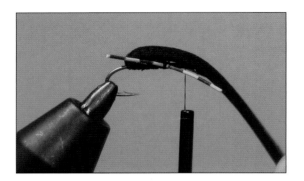

**Step 13:** Pull the foam strip forward and over the hook shank to make the beetle's shell.

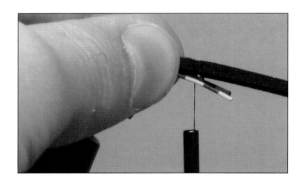

**Step 14:** Hold the foam in place on top of the hook and use a soft loop of thread over the foam and then pull strait down towards the tabletop to tighten the thread.

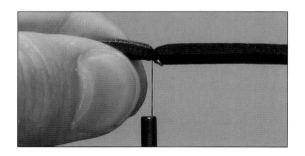

**Step 15:** Make several more tight thread wraps to secure the foam.

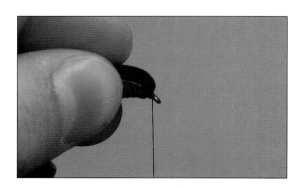

**Step 16:** Pull the front of the foam strip back so it folds over itself. Wrap thread in front of it to form the head.

**Step 17:** Whip finish the head.

**Step 18:** Trim the thread close to the head.

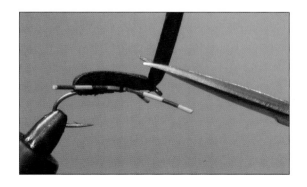

**Step 19:** Pull the end of the foam strip up and cut it with scissors so it's short and makes the head of the beetle. You can trim the rubber legs to the length you like.

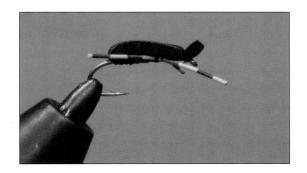

**Step 20:** Here is a side view of the finished beetle.

**Step 21:** This view shows the metallic foam back, which looks a lot like a real beetle.

I like to fish beetle patterns in high mountain streams during the summertime. It sure did the trick on this greenback cutthroat!

# Elk Hair Caddis

This is a very easy fly for beginners to tie, and it also teaches you some great techniques. The Elk Hair Caddis was not only the first hair-winged fly I ever tied, it was also the first dry fly that I fished and caught a fish on. I caught a rainbow trout.

It was sunny, and I was fishing some private ponds. I had been fishing all day with streamers and nymphs and hadn't caught a single fish! So, I decided to try something different. There had been some fish splashing and rising to bugs on the surface of the water. From what I could see it looked like they were caddisflies. Sometimes caddis will skitter or flutter on the surface and look like a small motor boat. When they are doing this the fish will sometimes make real loud splashy rises when they chase them down and eat them! Since this is what I had been watching, I decided to put on an Elk Hair Caddis. After a few minutes, I hooked a good-sized rainbow trout. It was about eighteen inches long and weighed around three pounds!

With the Elk Hair Caddis you can fish for many different species, including trout, bluegill, bass, and carp. This fly can be fished in lakes, ponds, streams, and rivers. In a pond or lake, the Elk Hair Caddis should either be stripped or left sitting still in the water. In a river or stream, you

## Elk Hair Caddis
### Material List

**Hook**
Tiemco 100 or Tiemco 9300

**Thread**
6/0, match color to body color

**Other materials**
Superfine dry fly dubbing, rooster saddle or neck hackle, fine ultra wire or copper wire, natural elk body hair, monofilament thread or 5X tippet material

want to cast the fly above you (upstream), and then let it swing downstream with a non-drag drift.

The techniques you'll learn are how to dub a dry-fly body, how to palmer a dry-fly hackle, how to stack elk hair to make a hair wing, and how to rib a body to keep it secure to the hook. You'll find these techniques useful in making other flies, too. The Elk Hair Caddis is a really fun fly to fish because it's always exciting to watch a fish eat a dry fly!

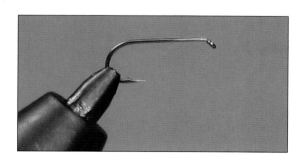

**Step 1:** Place the hook in the vise.

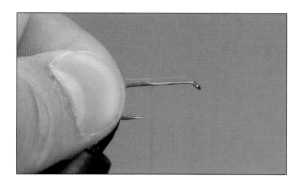

**Step 2:** Start the thread on the hook. Trim off the tag end of thread when you are done wrapping and tie on a piece of monofilament thread or 5X tippet material at about the middle of the hook.

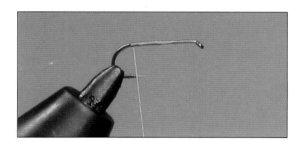

**Step 3:** Wrap back over the monofilament with the tying thread to the starting point.

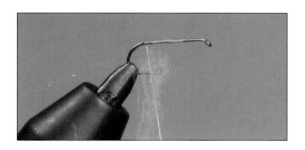

**Step 4:** Prepare some dry-fly dubbing by pulling it apart so it's fluffy. Then lay it on the tying thread so it can be rolled onto the thread.

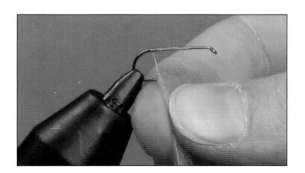

**Step 5:** Roll the dubbing and thread between your finger and thumb, creating a tight dubbing rope that will be the body of the fly. Remember to roll in one direction (not back and forth) at one spot on the dubbing, then move up or down the thread to tighten the dubbing at a different spot.

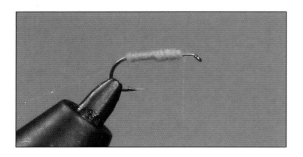

**Step 6:** Wrap the dubbing from the starting point forward until it is about two hook-eye lengths behind the eye. If you run out of dubbing on the tying thread, just repeat the dubbing process to add more onto the thread.

**Step 7:** Select a rooster saddle or rooster neck feather. A hackle gauge can be used to make sure it is the right size hackle feather for the hook size you are tying on. You can also buy packages of hackle that are already sized. These make it easy because you know you have the right size feather.

**Step 8:** Trim the fluffy stuff off the bottom of the quill, then trim a few hackle fibers from each side of the feathers' stem. It should look like a comb when you're done.

**Step 9:** Hold the hackle feather on your side of the hook and make a soft loop of thread over the stem, then tighten the loop.

**Step 10:** Make a few tight wraps of thread to secure the feather.

**Step 11:** Wrap the hackle back over the body (just like you did with the Woolly Bugger), making the spaces between the wraps equally spaced. This method of hackle wrapping is called palmering. Stop wrapping at the back of the body. Hackle pliers can be used to hold the feather, or you can hold it in your fingers. On really small flies, hackle pliers are very helpful!

**Step 12:** Use the piece of mono-filament to cross over the hackle feather, and then continue to spiral the monofilament over the hackle and the dubbed body to secure both to the hook.

**Step 13:** After you've reached the front of the body with the monofilament, cross over it with the tying thread. Continue with a few tight thread wraps to secure the monofilament.

**Step 14:** Cut the excess mono-filament close to the point it was secured with the thread wraps.

**Step 15:** Trim off the tip of the hackle feather at the back of the hook.

**Step 16:** Select a small clump of elk hair for the wing. It's better to have a smaller amount than too much hair. Start with less until it becomes easier for you to work with more hair.

**Step 17:** Cut the clump of hair off the hide. Always cut close to the hide so you can use the full length of the hair.

**Step 18:** Use a small comb, like this mustache comb, to comb out the soft underfur and short hair fibers. This is very important for making sure that the hair tips will be even in the hair stacker.

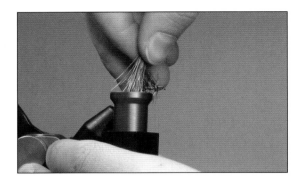

**Step 19:** Place the hair into the hair stacker with the uncut tips pointing down into the stacker.

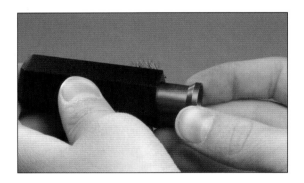

**Step 20:** Tap the stacker on the tabletop. It will sound like someone knocking on your door! The tapping evens all the hair tips on the bottom of the stacker. Now turn the stacker on its side and slowly pull the tube out of the stacker.

**Step 21:** Here's the stacker tube removed from the base and all the even elk hair tips sticking out so you can pinch them in your fingers to keep them even.

**Step 22:** Hold the hair, with the even tips pointing to the rear of the hook, on top of the shank to measure the wing length. I like to put the tips at the end of the body and pinch the hair right at the hook eye. This will measure the wing to be the length of the hook shank, which is a common length for dry fly wings.

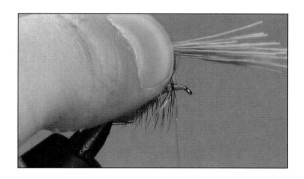

**Step 23:** Switch the hair into your other hand, making sure to keep the hair even and your measurement marked at the spot you were holding it. With the hair held slightly above the hook shank, make a full soft-loop around the elk hair only. This loop should not go around the hook shank.

**Step 24:** Now pull down slightly to sit the elk hair on the top of the hook and make another soft-wrap, this time around both the hair and the hook. Then pull straight down, keeping tight, even pressure on the thread. These thread wraps should be right in front of the dubbed body.

**Step 25:** Make eight to ten tight thread wraps at the same spot on the hair. When you're done, you can let go of the wing.

**Step 26:** Pull all the hair pointing over the hook eye back and make several wraps of thread in front of the hair. This will form the head and cause the hair to stand up away from the hook so it does not get into the hook eye.

**Step 27:** The wing is completed and the head is formed.

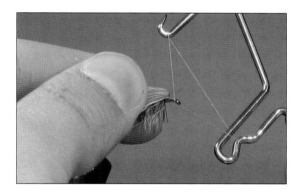

**Step 28:** Make a whip-finish knot to secure the thread wrap at the head. Cut off the tying thread close to the head of the fly.

**Step 29:** Pull the hair pointing over the hook eye straight up and cut straight with scissors. The hair should be trimmed about one hook-eye length above the thread wraps holding it in place. This crazy little tuft of hair looks kind of like the head of a real caddis fly.

**Step 30:** This is the finished Elk Hair Caddis. This will catch trout just about anywhere!

The Elk Hair Caddis is a great fly to fish when caddisflies are hatching. It is also a good dry fly to try when other things just aren't working. This brook trout gobbled it up!

# CDC Royal Trude

The first time I saw this fly was in a magazine called *Fly Tyer.* I said to myself, "Is that cool or what?" I went to my tying room and started to tie a couple of them. Just a few weeks later, I took it out to fish for green sunfish at Swietzer Lake. I caught some very nice fish that day with the CDC Royal Trude.

This is a great multi-purpose fly that can be fished in lakes, ponds, streams, and rivers. When you fish the CDC Royal Trude in lakes and ponds, you can strip it or let it stay still in the water. When you fish it in a stream or river, you want to let the fly swing downstream with a non-drag drift. This fly is a great multi-purpose fly that can be fished for many different types of fish. Some of the fish you can catch on a CDC Royal Trude are trout, bass, panfish, and carp.

## CDC Royal Trude
### Material List

**Hook**
Tiemco 9300 or Tiemco 5262

**Thread**
6/0, black

**Other materials**
golden pheasant tippet; peacock herl and red floss; dark brown rooster saddle or neck hackle; white CDC feathers

You'll learn some new techniques when you tie the CDC Royal Trude, like how to measure a good tail, how to wrap peacock herl to make bumps on the body, how to do a floss body, how to do a CDC wing, and how to wrap hackle to make a head. I like to fish this fly because it is a great all-around fly. I'll bet that you catch lots of fish on it!

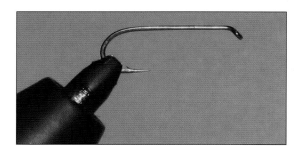

**Step 1:** Place the hook into the vise.

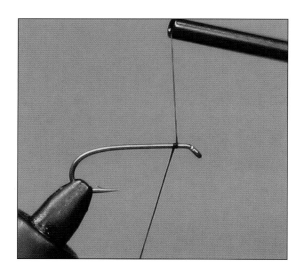

**Step 2:** Start tying the thread near the hook eye and then trim off the tag end of thread.

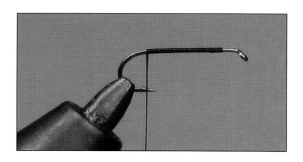

**Step 3:** Wrap the thread back toward the bend of the hook and stop at the starting point.

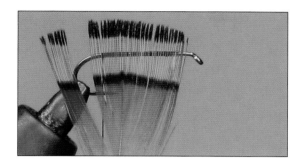

**Step 4:** Select a golden pheasant tippet feather to make the tail from.

**Step 5:** Separate a small number of fibers, making sure the tips are even, and cut them off of the center stem of the feather.

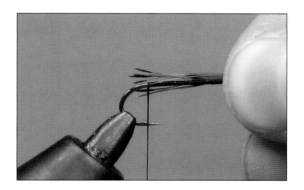

**Step 6:** Hold the feather fibers along the hook shank to measure the length of the tail. Most dry-fly tails should be about one shank length. I like to hold the tips of the fibers at the starting point and pinch the other end at the eye of the hook.

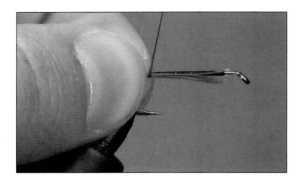

**Step 7:** Place the spot you pinched with your finger at the starting point so that the one shank-length of the fibers you measured is now sticking off the back of the hook to make the tail.

**Step 8:** Use the pinch-loop method to secure the tail on the top of the hook shank. Tie a couple of tight thread wraps to hold the tail in place.

**Step 9:** Wrap the tying thread forward over the fibers to the middle of the hook and cut off the excess fibers. Then wrap the tying thread back to where the tail is tied onto the hook. This makes an even underbody to wrap the finished body on top of.

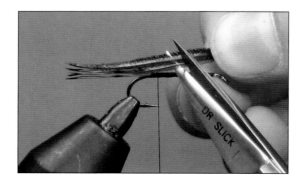

**Step 10:** Select three to four strands of peacock herl and trim their ends even with scissors.

**Step 11:** Using the pinch-loop method, secure the peacock herl at the rear of the hook right in front of the tail. Make a few thread wraps to cover up the ends of the peacock herl.

**Step 12:** Wrap the peacock herl around the shank three to four times so it makes a small bump, or ball, of herl. Cross over the herl with the tying thread and wrap forward toward the hook eye and over the herl.

**Step 13:** You'll use a short piece of red floss to make the red band in the body of this fly.

**Step 14:** With the tying thread, make a couple of thread wraps over the red floss, securing it to the hook in front of the ball of peacock.

**Step 15:** Pull backwards on the red floss, and it will slide the tag end of the floss back towards the tie-in point so you don't have to cut it off with your scissors. Make sure to check that the floss is tied right in front of the peacock ball.

**Step 16:** Begin to wrap the red floss forward. The floss should be wrapped about the same length as the peacock ball at the beginning of the body.

**Step 17:** When it has been wrapped the correct distance, cross over the floss with the tying thread and secure it with a few tight wraps of thread.

**Step 18:** Cut off the excess red floss and wrap the thread so it is in front of the long strand of peacock.

**Step 19:** Wrap the strands of peacock forward to form the second bump of peacock herl. The body will be made up of equal thirds (peacock, red floss, and peacock).

**Step 20:** Cross over the strands of peacock herl with the tying thread and secure it with a few wraps of thread. Then cut off the excess peacock herl.

**Step 21:** Use two to three white CDC feathers for the wing. Hold the CDC feathers on top of the hook to measure the length of the wing. I hold the tips at the starting point and pinch the other ends at the hook eye so the wing measures about one hook shank length.

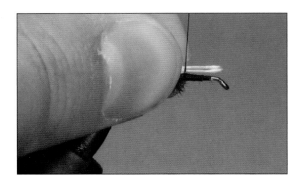

**Step 22:** Move the ends pinched in your fingers so they are right in front of the second peacock herl bump. Hold the wing with your other hand and use a pinch-loop to secure the feathers on top of the hook to make the wing.

**Step 23:** Make a few tight wraps to hold the wing feathers to the hook.

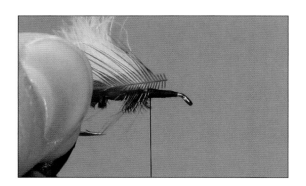

**Step 24:** Trim off the excess ends of the wing feathers close to the hook shank and select a dry-fly hackle that is the correct size for the hook you are tying on. Trim off the soft fuzzy stuff at the bottom of the feather and trim a few fibers on each side of the stem (this is the same way the Elk Hair Cadis hackle feather was trimmed and prepared).

**Step 25:** Tie the hackle feather in on your side of the hook with the shinny side facing toward you.

**Step 26:** Hold the hackle feather with your fingers or in a hackle pliers and begin to wrap the hackle toward the hook eye.

**Step 27:** Stop wrapping the feather a short distance behind the eye of the hook and cross over the feather with the tying thread, making several tight wraps to secure it firmly to the hook.

**Step 28:** The hackle is finished being wrapped and this is what it should look like.

**Step 29:** Cut the excess hackle feather off as close as possible to the shank of the hook.

**Step 30:** Make a few wraps of thread to form a smooth head and whip-finish the fly.

**Step 31:** Cut off the tying thread.

**Step 32:** This is one neat finished fly!

The CDC Royal Trude will catch trout and bass, but it is also very useful for catching panfish, like this bluegill.

# 8 Wrapping it All Up!

You know, fly tying is not all about the flies. It's also about learning how to use new materials, getting to go to new places, and meeting new people. I've met many new people at various fly-tying shows, and they've shown me that you can get really creative with fly tying. One of them, Jens Pilgaard, who lives in Denmark, taught me how to tie a salmon fly in my hands without a vise or bobbin. All he used were his hands, a dubbing needle, scissors, and a length of thread. This is how the early fly tiers tied flies. Another friend of mine, Jay "Fishy" Fullum, uses all kinds of off-the-wall crazy materials like coffee stir sticks, craft store ribbon, and even the foam trays that meat is packaged in at the grocery store! He even uses a strike indicator that is cut into fourths to make a popper head. There are so many different ways to tie flies, why not try to make your

Foam bee, tied by Bill Logan.

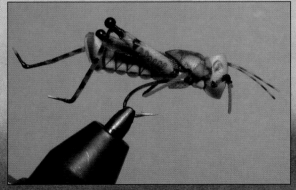

Realistic grasshopper, tied by Bill Logan.

own special way of doing it? Now let's look at some different fly patterns so you can get some ideas for tying new flies.

Fishy's Hopper is a neat, fun fly. Tied by Fishy Fullum.

Fishy's Itsy Bitsy Spider, tied by Fishy Fullum.

My good friend Jens and I tied this Atlantic salmon fly together. We didn't use a bobbin or a vise. I once watched him tie this fly by himself at a fly-tying show in New Jersey. It took him six hours!

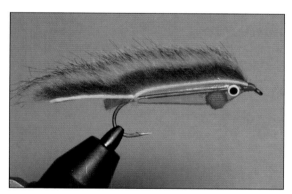

Theo's Hot Melt streamer, tied by Theo Bakelaar.

Here is a streamer that my friend David Gourang from Norway tied. David uses this fly for catching pike. They like to eat big streamer flies.

Polish or Czech Nymph, tied by Valadi Trzebuni.

Valadi Nymph with buggy body and a gold bead head, tied by Valadi Trzebuni.

I was very fortunate to be able to take a class with Valadi to learn the weaving techniques he uses to tie most of his flies.

Valadi helping me with some tying techniques at a show.

Jay "Fishy" Fullum has shown and taught me a lot about different materials. Some of the things he uses are crazy. He uses one of those Styrofoam trays that meat is sold in at the grocery store to tie a baby bluegill pattern. He also uses plastic coffee stir sticks to extend bodies on flies! Fishy writes fly tying articles for *Fly Tyer* magazine. Look for his articles because they are so much fun and teach you about some great flies.

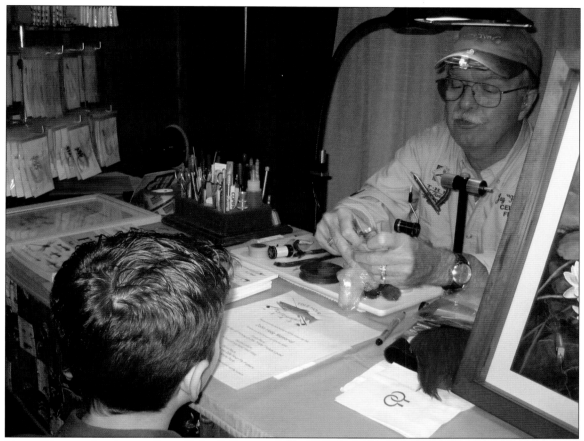

Me getting a tying lesson from Fishy Fullum at a fly-tying show in Texas.

This is Chappie Chapman. I met him at a show in Pasadena, California. He has been tying flies for more than 60 years! He shared a lot of information about the foam flies he was tying there that day.

Bill Logan from New Jersey giving me some important pointers about tying a realistic stonefly nymph.

Will Travis showing and explaining his method for tying a fly called the Kiwi Muddler at a show in Arlington, Texas.

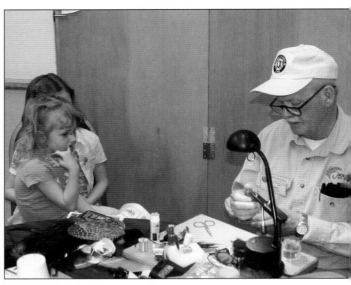

Bob Jacklin from West Yellowstone, Montana, showing my sisters Ava and Vivian how to tie his March Brown Nymph at a fly-tying show in Grand Junction, Colorado.

You can make fly tying as simple or as complicated as you want. There are so many different styles of fly tying that you can try, from the simplest patterns like the San Juan Worm, to the most complicated realistic flies, like some of Paul Willock's stonefly nymphs and adults. Those can take many, many hours to complete.

If you get really into tying flies, there are many fly-tying competitions that you can enter flies into. I just entered my first two competitions this year. I entered into the junior division in both. That means I only had to compete against kids sixteen years old and under. One competition that I entered was the British and International Fly-Tying Championships. The other was the Mustad Scandinavian Fly-Tying Competition. They award certificates and sometimes medals if your flies place high in the competition. I hope more kids participate in these fun contests. They are a very good way to have someone else (the judging panel of expert tiers) give you feedback about your fly-tying skills. All this will just help improve your tying abilities.

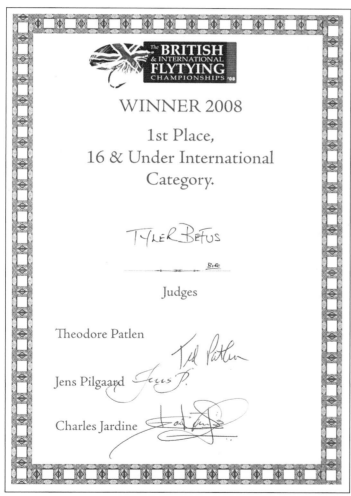

This is the first place certificate I received for winning the 2008 British and International Fly-Tying Championships Junior Division.

This is the silver medal I won for second place in the 2008 Mustad Scandinavian Open Junior Division.

It is fun showing kids, like this group of boys, how to tie their first fly.

I like to demonstrate and talk to kids at their schools and introduce them to fly tying so that maybe some of them will start to tie flies.

My whole family likes to tie flies. Being able to sit next to my dad and show kids and adults how to tie flies is a great way to spend time together.

It's also a lot of fun to tie flies at the large fly-fishing shows where there are many people watching you and asking questions so they can learn more.

Collecting flies from different fly tiers is just another fun part of the whole activity of fly tying. I enjoy collecting and swapping flies with my friends, family, and different fly tiers I meet at shows and events. Some of the flies have been pictured throughout this book, but I also wanted to show you a gallery of different flies from different fly tiers, including some more flies that I have tied. Seeing different flies and how different materials can be used helps me to be more creative with my own fly tying. I hope some of these flies will inspire you to try new things and most of all have *fun* tying flies. Anything is possible when you are having fun!

Yankee Wet Fly, tied by Tyler Befus.

Royal Coachman Wet Fly, tied by Tyler Befus.

CDC Cranefly Adult, tied by Tyler Befus.

Origami Wing Emerger, tied by Jen Pilgaard.

Dun Quill Dry Fly, tied by Tyler Befus.

Flying Black Ant, tied by Brad Befus.

Quill Gordon Dry Fly, tied by Tyler Befus.

BC Hopper, tied by Charlie Craven.

WaterWisp Mayfly, tied by Dick Talluer.

Ladybug, tied by Bob Mead.

Wired Stone Nymph, tied by Brad Befus.

Realistic Stonefly Nymph, tied by Bill Logan.

Woven Polish Nymph, tied by Tyler Befus.

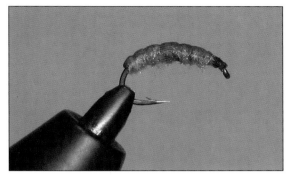

Czech Nymph, tied by Brad Befus.

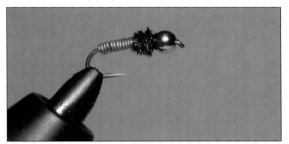

Hot Pink Bead Head Brassie, tied by Ava Befus.

Realistic Caddis Larva, tied by Tyler Befus.

Tyler's Fakey Nymph, tied by Tyler Befus.

March Brown Nymph, tied by Bob Jacklin.

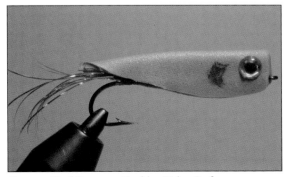

Crease Fly Minnow, tied by Tyler Befus.

Squirrel Streamer, tied by Tyler Befus.

Tyler's Electric Leech, tied by Tyler Befus.

Tyler's Secret Weapon, tied by Tyler Befus.

Cone Head Rabbit Streamer, tied by Tyler Befus.

Soft Hackle Baitfish, tied by Tyler Befus.

Marabou Minnow, tied by Tyler Befus.

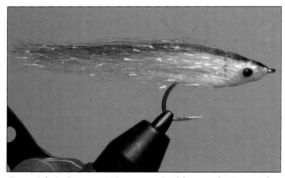

Gartside's Secret Minnow, tied by Jack Gartside.

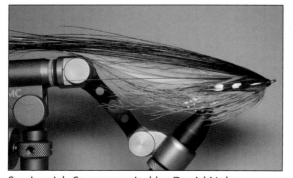

Squimpish Streamer, tied by David Nelson.

Rainbow Trout Streamer, tied by Jay Murakoshi.

D's Minnow, tied by Brad Befus.

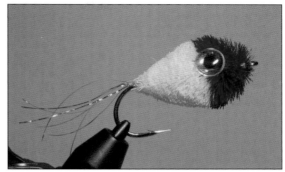

Bobble Head, tied by Tyler Befus.

Deer Hair Diver, tied by Tyler Befus.

Deer Hair Pike, tied by Tim Jacobs.

Deer Hair Frog, tied by Billy Munn.

Deer Hair Mouse, tied by Billy Munn.

CB Shad, tied by Jay Murakoshi.

CB Baitfish, tied by Jay Murakoshi.

Sili Grub, tied by Brad Befus.

Bonefish Shrimp, tied by Will Travis.

Saltwater Shrimp, tied by Ken Hanley.

Green Butt Skunk, tied by Brad Befus.

Spey Style Fly, tied by Tyler Befus.

Popsicle, tied by Tyler Befus.

Night Hawk, tied by Brad Befus.

Soft Hackle Hares Ear, tied by Tyler Befus.

I hope you've enjoyed this book and I hope you've learned something from it. **Now let's tie some flies!**

A box of flies ready to help you catch fish and have fun.

Tyler Befus may only be eleven years old, but he has already been flyfishing and tying his own flies for more than eight years. He is the youngest member of the Ross Reels, Rio Products, Inc., Oakley, Simms Fishing Products, and Whiting Farms pro staff teams and is a Signature Fly designer for Umpqua Feather Merchants. He currently holds International Game Fish Association Junior World Records for sheefish and Kokanee salmon. Tyler's fly-tying abilities have been honored with a first place finish in the 2008 British and International Fly Tying Championships 16 and under International Category, and a Silver Medal winner in the 2008 Mustad Scandinavian Open Fly Tying Competition Junior Division. Tyler's first book, *A Kids Guide to Flyfishing,* was released in 2006.